EART

A Seasonal Guide to
the Old Religion

By Margaret McArthur
Edited by Julia & Jon Day

EARTH MAGIC
A Seasonal Guide to the Old Religion

©1994 Margaret McArthur, Julia Day & Jon Day

Cover & internal illustrations by Gill Bent
Cover design by Daryth Bastin

Published by:

Capall Bann Publishing
Freshfields
Chieveley
Berks
RG16 8TF

Dedication

To
Gladys & John

and

David - my long suffering non-pagan husband!

Contents

Note From the Editors

If you are looking for a 'ritual recipe book' - a tome of set words and actions to reel off at the appropriate time of year, this is not the book for you.

Margaret MacArthur has a deep-rooted feeling for the Craft and has dictated this book straight from the heart. Instead of reeling off high-sounding words and 'Rupert Bear' style poetry, Margaret concentrates on encouraging the reader to really take notice of the seasons - the ebbs and flows of nature and to explore how they affect us.

Simple ideas and homely wisdom are presented here encouraging us all to develop ourselves, to become truly part of, and at one with, the natural things around us and care for the earth - linking us with the real magic and spirituality of the old Craft. Reading this book you realise that it is not the words of a ritual which are important, it is the feeling, concentration and intent behind them.

Apart from her deep love of the Craft, Margaret is renowned in pagan circles for her great love of cooking and she has included a number of traditional recipes to give the reader a real taste of the traditional Craft.

Julia & Jon Day

Foreword

When I was first asked to write this book, I sat down and I thought, "What can I write about?" The only thing I can write about is that which I know. That which I know, is knowledge that has been passed down to me about life, about what we believe in, about the ground beneath our feet and the sun in the sky, about feelings, places, love.

I hope that you find this book useful and that it will answer questions and help you grow within.

There are recipes that have been passed down to me, there are sayings, information, all sorts of things! I have tried to make it a guide to what is around you. This book is NOT about high magic rituals or how to draw pentagrams in the sky! What it is about, is going to find an oak tree and finding the energy of that tree and making your peace with it.

Natural magic is one of the oldest pathways, but it is one that has been forgotten by so many, because people want glitz and glamour, not mud! But in that mud, there are the most beautiful jewels and gems that you will ever find, because you will find the spirit of the place and the spirit within your own soul. That is what makes natural magic different. That is what makes it, that which is THERE.

We do not use tools that are foreign to the land, but we use the tools OF the land. We walk our pathway, although it is a long and difficult one, but at the end of it, we have more joy and more laughter. We work outside amongst the trees and the fields, on the hills and where the spirit of the land can be found.

This is my way and I hope that you find it interesting and of value.

Every word that has been written, has been written with love and I hope to teach you a story of tomorrow.

Blessed be and blessed be the pathway you follow and the steps that you take.

Margaret McArthur

Introduction

To anyone who has picked up this book, this is the part of the book that tells you what is inside. Inside is a journey, a journey to a way of life, a journey of thoughts, of time and of laughter, a journey of love, of spiritual love and of love for fellow man.

I hope that this book will teach you a new way of love, will show you a new pathway that can be walked, a new time in your life. If you put down this book now, then I would say goodbye to you, but if pick this book up and take it home, then I say,

"Welcome, to the path of the Lord and Lady. Blessed Be."

The Beginning

Imagine if you will, a glade lit by moonlight on a winters night with snow on the ground. A group of people standing with hands linked, a priestess and priest standing together with love. The priestess says the opening words that will make the circle one. As she calls forth the elements with the priest, working together as one, there you have the start, the start for any Wiccan circle, a group of people who have come together.

Magic is not all about spells and paraphernalia. Love; love for the God and Goddess, love for the trees, the grass, the whole of nature and the spirits around you. A feeling for and understanding of the elements that make up the world. A great deal of that has been lost in modern day magic. People have gone more for the rituals in their living rooms rather than going outside to feel the grass beneath their feet and the wind in their hair.

Many parts of the pathway call upon different names of gods and goddesses. They call upon the name of a river in a god, but surely each river does not have the same name. If you wish to know the names of a river, go and ask it.

I'll try to explain how this is done. Feel what is around you, what is always there and will always be there as long as we maintain to look after the earth. In the beginning man had no names for the gods, he worshipped the ground beneath his feet, the sun and moon in the sky, the wind and elements. For many Wiccans this is still true, those are the things we worship, there are no names for those things, they are there, they always have been and they always will be.

So join that circle, feel the warmth of the hand next to yours and grasp it. Join in that circle that they hold at the full moon glade and hear the Lady's words: "Welcome to me my children, come into the circle, come join hand in hand, dance under the full moon and cry with joy for my love is with you". Hear the priest declaim "Sons and daughters, I look upon you, you are my life, my spirit, I live in you as you live in me".

Feel the beat and the rhythm as the circle starts its winding journey to the centre of life. On many occasions I've been in moonlit glades, I've witnessed and felt people around me dancing in the full moon, but what does it mean? Why are they there? They are there because each and every one of them, within themselves, have taken into account the God and Goddess in their lives. They have realised that there is male and female in both sexes, the balance of life.

To have real balance you must have both the male and female, one can not exist without the other. A child can not be born by one alone, it takes two to make a child, to make life. This is very, very important for all the work that you will do in the Craft. The first step is to become one with yourself, to look at what you are is the hardest thing you can ever do. It is the hardest thing anyone can do. Look at yourself, look at the things that may let you down in life.

I'm not saying you have to be perfect. Nobody is. All I'm saying is that you should look at your faults and realise that other people have their faults too. To be more patient, more understanding, that is one of the major things I have learnt through the worship of what I hold dear. Patience is an excellent, though difficult, thing to have.

The God and Goddess

Let us look at the God and Goddess. The Goddess symbol is the earth. The ground beneath our feet, the trees, everything that exists here. The God symbol is the sun. Without the sun, the Lord, no plant would grow upon the surface of the earth, no tree would reach expectantly into the wind. None of this would be there. So together they work as one and weave their spell with the moon, the governor of the tides. Many link strongly with the moon, females especially, with her waxing and waning. I'll go into more detail later on as to why and how this is. Without any of these the world as we know it would not exist. The sun gives us warmth during the day and the moon the time of rest at night that plants and animals need. So now you see the circle, the Lord and the Lady, and the Daughter as the moon is sometimes looked upon.

Now go back to the glade, the glade I first took you to. The people there are growing tired, they are nearing the ending of the rite and the circle is closing. But as their circle closes it may open something up in you. Think about what I have said. Think about how the Lord and Lady act together, the earth and the sun, how they govern your everyday life and what they do in that life, because in the end that is what we are worshipping; all that is around us. The Lord and Lady are in all of us and in all of nature.

The Goddess, the Lady

The goddess is sometimes seen as having three aspects; the Maiden, the Mother and the Crone. The Maiden is the virgin, purity, clarity of thought, the beginning of life and the beginning of the cycle of life.

I can remember the first time that I went to the Goddess and said,"Lady, you are my life."

The Three Stages of Womanhood

The Maiden

I can remember when I first walked on the pathway, when I was a Maiden, pure of mind and body and spirit. (Well one is meant to be anyway - and I was, once!). The Maiden is purity and clarity. She is the first stage of womanhood. There are many things that we forget now about that stage of our life, such as innocence. Nowadays young girls seem to want to lose their innocence far too soon.

There is a celebration in the Craft for the time when a girl reaches her first menstrual cycle. Many different religions do this when the child is becoming a woman. I think we forget that not so long ago, many girls were married at the age of 14. They were seen as young women.

The ceremony itself is a very beautiful one, where all the women come together. They take her off and bathe her and give her a very plain dress and put flowers in her hair and celebrate the fact that she is now a woman and no longer a child.

That is only one aspect of Maidenhood. The Maidens' part in a circle is that of helper and supporter to the priestess, assisting the priestess in her work. Many priestesses would not be able to continue their work without the help of their circle maiden.

The Maidens' duties are many and varied, from helping run the circle itself, to making sure that there are candles and that the incense is ready by making it up before the rite itself. Her job is varied in many ways. It is her time of learning. It is a time of waiting until she becomes a priestess herself.

There are two ways in which the Maiden may take the next step. One is that she is accepted as a priestess or, she gets married and has a child. This takes her on to the next stage, that of the Mother.

The Mother

The Mother is precisely that. The Mother who gives, she who tends and nurtures the children.

Motherhood, the stage before Eldership, is the time of fertility. It is the time when women are in their childbearing years. This does not just apply to childbirth, for during this time women are at their height whether they have children or not. Usually within a circle a woman has to be of childbearing age to represent the Goddess as the priestess because the Goddess is the symbol and very essence of female fertility.

The Mother is the priestess, she is the mother of our lives, she is the celebration of motherhood. Within the circle, she is not only the mother to her children, but also the mother to the circle. She is the one that the children, the followers of the Lord and Lady can go to for help with any problems or troubles that they have within the circle itself.

The Mother is the Earth beneath our feet. She is alive. She is full of love for her children, therefore she is someone to be respected and loved. Therefore, the position of the priestess is one of love and respect.

The priestess herself, though, has many responsibilities. She has the responsibility of teaching and passing on knowledge to the children. She also has the job of being Mother to the circle, meaning that she leads the circle in ritual. She calls upon the four elements with the priest. Her responsibility is a very grave one and one which should never be taken lightly. It is a very heavy responsibility.

The Mother is also she who gives birth, not only to her own children, but to ideas. She will plant the seed of an idea within someone's head and help them to nurture it, to help it to grow and to aid that person in fulfilling their fullest points of life.

If you know a person who can write beautiful words or music, but is too afraid to take the first step of writing, then surely it is your duty to help them. Not to say, "You must", but to encourage them to show that you understand the beauty in their soul and to help them that way.

It is not a position to be misused. It is a position of help and love.

There are people though, who use the position for their own means and not that of the mother. I think that sometimes they forget that they are answerable to the Mother herself. They are her servants. I remember when I used to lay down before any time that I ever did a ritual. I used to lay in front of the altar and I used to say, "Mother, I am your servant, do with me as thou wilt for you are my life." Then I used to get up and work for her. I fully believed that when I did the ritual, or whatever else I was doing, I was doing it for her. I was taking on her shadow, becoming her for that time.

After the stages of Motherhood, after the children are grown, one of the hardest things for any mother, is to let go. So it is for any priestess. The hardest thing when a member of your circle is ready to leave to form their own circle, is to let go. You should always do so, because, if you hold them back, you hold them back from their destiny. To do that would be wrong. Everyone has their own time and their own destiny.

The Crone

The Crone is the wisewoman, not the deathbringer, but the wisewoman, she who has wisdom in her hands. Today there is little respect for the old. They may have many years of wisdom and experience, yet all too often this is ignored. In times gone by this was not the case, the old people were respected in their own right for their wisdom and knowledge. That is something we have lost today, something that is sadly lacking in our society. Perhaps it is time to rethink this, to ask and see what knowledge they have. I think a lot of people would be surprised if they really talked to the older people around them.

In my own experience, in a circle when a person reached retiring age they were not just put on the scrap heap and told 'We don't want you anymore'. They reached the status of Eldership. Becoming an Elder of the circle is a very well thought of position. As an Elder they would be approached for advice and information drawn from their years of experience which would benefit the other circle members.

Now let us look at all three aspects together, the Goddess in all her stages. We can look at the reflection of these in the seasons. The Maiden for spring, the time of purity and promise. The summer being the fertile fruitful time when the burgeoning earth swells with the harvest, the time of the Mother. The dark months of winter being the time of the Crone, the time of rest and preparation for the rebirth of spring. All three have their part in life, all three their balance of the seasons.

I mentioned earlier that the moon is a symbol that reflects womanhood. Many women who join the Craft find that their menstrual cycle links with the moon, changing as they become more in tune with the flows of life and what is around them in nature. If this happens to you, don't worry, it is quite normal.

The God, the Lord

Now we have looked at the feminine principal, let us look at the masculine. In many ways the sun god has taken a back seat in many circles. He is not given the reverence that is due to him except at the Midsummer and Midwinter Solstices. A lot of people forget that the male is as strong and important a figure in the Craft as the female. This is a natural reaction against the patriarchal society that most of us have been brought up in. But the God is as important as the Goddess, the two are equal and essential.

Lord. Herne the Hunter. Lord of the Woods. He is the Green Man, the Wild One, he is Herne, he is all these things. The mate of the priestess, the mate of the Mother. You cannot make a child with only one sex. You need a mother and a father, male and female, not just to make the child, but for the child to be balanced and to have a balanced life.

I do not believe that you can have a priestess without a priest. They both work together. I am not saying that two homosexuals cannot work together, but why on Earth cannot a gay man and a gay woman come together if they both feel the Lord and Lady in their spirit?

Both should always be equal, as there is feminine within us, so there is masculine. Where there is masculine, there is feminine.

In times gone by, when a boy came to manhood, he was given a bow and arrow and taken on his first hunt, to hunt his first stag. That was the sign of his manhood.

When the Lord first comes to the Lady, when they both mate, the priest and priestess join as one. Together they are the symbol of the Great Rite. The Great Rite being the joining of the Lord and Lady. The ceremony is usually only done between a priest and priestess who are married or a couple who have made a commitment to each other. It is very rare for two people who are not an established couple to do the Great Rite. It is a symbol of unity. You could not do the Great Rite, without the priest, without the man, without the Green Man.

In many circles the priestess takes charge, the priest does not have much work to do. I believe this is wrong and unbalanced and should not be. If we look at the male mythology we see Herne, the Green Man, Father Oak and many other aspects, all these govern the masculine.

The stag is an important symbol in the craft, the symbol of Herne or Cernunnos. Do we need names? To many of us he is simply the Horned One, the Lord. Others use names to link with certain aspects at particular times of year, or for particular rites; for instance Herne the leader of the Wild Hunt at Samhain.

The important thing to look at is how the two principles, male and female, fit into your life. Many people consider that the female governs the emotions while the male rules the logical thought processes. I do not agree with that outlook. We all have both male and female in our make-up and we have to come to terms and balance both sides. As you step deeper into the Craft the importance of this will become more apparent, enabling you to look more closely at, and relate to, what is around you.

The Elements

Earth, air, fire and water; the basic elements of nature, each one is essential to our existence and each has a major impact in our lives. The air we breathe, the fire which gives us warmth, the water that sustains all life and the earth that provides the food we eat. These elements are also the basics of earth magic. Let us look at them individually and see how they work in our lives.

Earth

Earth can be many things. Destructive forces? Think of a landslide! Many of you may remember, or have heard about, the disaster in the sixties, when there was a landslide from a coalpit spoil heap that buried the school in Aberfan in Wales and destroyed so many young lives. People asked themselves afterwards why they had not done anything about it. Most probably they did not think that there was any danger. It was caused by the combination of earth and water. Landslides happen all over the world, even in places where people think there is no danger.

Look at what happens when fire and earth combine, to form the force and fury of a volcano. You have molten earth, lava, molten rock. A volcano is a thing that can make a new island, a new life. It can also destroy livelihoods and the lives of men when it goes down the side of a hill.

Think of the sheer force that earth has. It gives us our food. We grow our food in it, we grow our life in it. We take resources from it, coal, gas, oil, all these things come from earth.

Look at how much you rely upon the products of earth in your everyday life. There is that which you eat and that which you sit upon, which is made from wood usually. Wood comes from trees which grow from the earth. All these things you rely upon.

We should never underestimate earth. How much of it will be left in the future if we go on consuming it in the way that we do? I do not think that there will be a lot.

Earth, the very ground beneath our feet. How to get in touch with earth? One way is to perform a very simple working. What I want you to do is to find a place, a place that to you particularly symbolises the earth. Whether it is a cavern, the side of an ancient burial mound, a rocky grotto in a local park or simply part of your own garden. Go to that special place, where you feel closest to the earth, put out your hand and touch the ground. Start to really feel it, its texture, moisture, smell, all its characteristics. Imagine you are entering it, perhaps as a mole. Feel the earth on your skin, drier and crumbly on the surface, moist and dark as you enter it. Feel that you are part of the earth, becoming one with it. Now gradually come out and feel the beat of the earth, it does have a heartbeat, the living pulse of the Lady. Feel it, it's there.

Don't be worried or disappointed if you can not make the link at the first attempt. The more you go back to that place the more you will get to know it and the more it will get to know you, making it easier to work there and to feel the earth. We have many senses, use all of them. Don't just feel the earth with your hands, smell it, listen to it. The idea is to stretch out and really use all your senses, to break out of the bonds forced on them by modern living.

To do this working I have often taken people to West Kennet Longbarrow or Waylands Smithy. These are just two examples of strong earth places. There are many more scattered throughout the country.

As I said, earth can be many things. It is our home and the provider of the food we eat. It can be a safe haven or an immensely powerful force; look at the power in an earthquake, a volcano or a mudslide - immense unstoppable power.

Air

You could just say 'we breathe it', but there is much more to air than that. Go to an airy place - an open moor or the top of a hill on a windy day. Stretch your arms up and feel the force of the wind. Air can be a cooling breeze of a summers day or the destructive maelstrom of a hurricane sweeping all before it.

Let us look at the two levels of air. As air is a soothing breeze, it is also a hurricane. I think sometimes as a race, we underestimate the power of air, the force and power of a hurricane, of a typhoon. All these things are related to and part of air.

You have the wildness of air and the stillness of air, still one, still part of the same thing. You will find in your work later on that you will need to understand both sides, both the calmness and the wildness of air.

You must not forget the cool breeze of a warm summer's day which gently caresses your body and soothes it and cools it, because that is also part of air.

When you find that airy spot to do the bird meditation that follows, I also want you to visit it, taking a kite with you, or just a piece of cloth. Go to the top of the hill and feel the strength of the wind on yourself and on the kite or piece of cloth. It will help you understand just how much strength there is in the wind and how much strength is there for you to be part of.

Take yourself to a place of air, preferably on a day when there

is some movement, but not too windy. Stand, or sit, personally I have found it better to stand for this working, and relax. Feel the air about you, feel it move and caress you.

Stretch out your arms, feel them change, becoming lighter, transforming into wings. Your body is changing shape, sprouting feathers, your eyes keener, your senses sharper, you are a bird. Take your first step, unfurl your wings, make your first tentative movements, testing the air. Now launch yourself from the ground.

Do not worry of you have problems at first, many people do. What sort of of bird are you? A hawk, a stately swan, or flittering sparrow? Ride the currents and flows of the air, feel it taking you higher and higher, hover for a brief while. Savour the freedom as you soar through the air. Then swoop down, back towards the earth. Land on the ground and gradually lose your feathers, your wings become arms once more and you are yourself again.

It is a very wonderful experience, but as I say if it does not work first time, don't be discouraged, just try again. With practice you will gradually get there. It is one of the best ways that I know of finding air.

Try to make the time to keep a diary for a week and see how air and wind have effected things around you. See what effect it has. Do not forget that wind can destroy a crop. It can hurl the sea over a sea wall. It is a very very strong element. Never underestimate it.

Fire

Fire too has many aspects, the gentleness of a candle, the ferociousness of the forest fire, the warmth and security of a fire in the hearth. These are all part of fire. If you have space in your back garden, it is an idea to build a bonfire and to just look at it and feel it, become part of it. Look at how it dances and look at the shadows that it makes. Look into it. Be careful not to burn yourself!

That is fire's tendency, to burn, to consume. A small fire can soon become a big one, given dry wood, or other fuel, it can so easily become a terrifying force to be contended with. Man has never fully controlled fire. It still has that uncontrollable air about it. We think that we have control of it and then all of a sudden it will flare up. It will just go whoosh! Then it can become a forest fire. A cigarette, an ember, can lead from smoke to flame to destruction in such a brief time. That is the part of fire that we do not often think of, the destructive force.

Fire can be used in the Craft for a wide variety of magical workings, from healing to destroying. It is a tremendously powerful element and, possibly more than all the other elements, must be used with care. Fire can burn, it can destroy, but it can also heal and purify. It can be the comforting candle flame in the darkness, the warming flame in the cold, the engulfing furnace of the forest fire, even the healing tool of medical laser treatment. When you think of fire, think of its many uses.

The meditation for this element is really quite simple in many ways. When you are meditating, when you are going from your candle flame, your small flame and then increasing it, remember, you must always keep control. You must always stay there, you must always keep control of your mind. It is always best to leave the fire meditation to be the last meditation that you do.

I want you to imagine a candle flame. A very small flame in the dark. Feel the comforting warmth the flame gives off as you extend your hands towards it. As your hands near it they will merge with the flame, you become one, you are the flame,

incandescent in the darkness. Then I want you to gradually build up your flame,to the size of a bonfire. Gradually picture it in your mind, growing larger and larger until you have that fire there, a blazing mound of light and heat. Then I want you to stop and gradually reduce back down to the comforting ambience of the candle flame - feel the glow of homely warmth.

If it helps you to actually light a candle and have that in front of you, do so by all means, but be very careful. When you have brought this bonfire back in your mind down to a candle flame then leave it. Come back to it another day and do it again, but this time make your flame larger than a bonfire. Do not get too carried away, because otherwise fire can get out of control. Feel the potential for destruction, but you must learn to control it and bring it back down again. When you put your candle flame there, look at it and feel it.

Many healers say that when they heal people,the palms of their hands become very warm and they can feel where a person is injured by the amount of heat that the body is giving off in that area. They feel the heat in the palms of their hands growing stronger over the place that needs healing. The person who is being healed says that the place where they are being healed is getting warmer, but it is a soothing, healing warmth. So there is that sort of warmth from fire. At the other end of the scale there is also the raging destructive wave of a forest fire.

Again, as with earth, keep a diary during a week to see how fire actually exists. Do not forget, fire is in an electric bulb, in the sun above you and in your own passions. It is all around you. So keep that diary and look at it afterwards to see how fire is in your life.

Water

Now we come to water. Water can be a stream, flowing, trickling down the side of a mountain, it can be a still pond reflecting the landscape around it or perhaps the sea itself, raging, deep and strong. When you think about the sea, think about all the creatures that live in it. Think about what is there, beneath the surface.

Without water we could not live. We ourselves are made out of a great deal of water. Look how water affects the female at the full moon. Look at how we ourselves react if we cannot have enough. It is something that we just cannot do without. The human body can go far longer without food than it can survive without water. Without water, we can survive for three or four days, without food, for a week or even longer. We need water desperately, not just for ourselves, but for the animals around us and the plants around us.

Look at what happens in a heat wave, even in this country renowned for its rain. Look at what happens to the earth, because it is not used to being without water, cracks appear in it. The earth cracks up and dries out and plants gradually begin to die through lack of water.

Also consider the force and energy that water has. A tidal wave can wipe out a village. Think how it combines with the other elements. Earth and water become a mud slide. Combine water with fire and you have steam. The first trains ran on steam, as did many things at the start of the industrial revolution.

The elements combine in different ways and can either be used as a good force, or as a force for destruction.

We get a lot of our electricity from water, using hydro dams. There are other ways to use it for the good.

The exercise for water is to find a nice quiet place beside a river or other moving water. Begin by looking at the river. Look at how it is flowing, fast or slow, deep or shallow, clear or obscure. Look around you and see what lives in the river, the fishes, insects and plants. Think about how vital water is to life. Gradually look into the river. Find a fish. Imagine that you are a fish in that river. Imagine that you are swimming along it, feeling the force and energy of the river around you.

If you can get into the river, great. If you can get in and feel what is actually there, but do not put yourself in danger. If it is paddling across a river, then fine, or if it is a river that you can swim in safely but remember, whatever you do, do not put yourself in danger whilst doing this exercise. I want you to gradually feel the water that is around you, if it is just putting your hand in by reaching down from the bank and feeling the water ripple through your fingers.

I want you to imagine that you are that fish in that river swimming along it either with the current or against the current. Feel the eddies around you. If you cannot get to a river, but you can get to the sea, then go to the sea and feel the force of the waves against your body, feel the waves coming in and out, feeling the force of the current going around you and coming around you. If you cannot get to either of these then find a pond or anything of that nature, so you can be near it while you are doing the exercise. Try and feel it around you.

As I have said, we must never underestimate any of the elements at all.

Conclusion of meditations on the elements

At the end of these meditations, when you have done them, you will have become more in touch with the elements, I hope, and you will have seen how much they affect your life, your everyday being. That is the first step to understanding what is around you. You cannot fully understand the seasons or what changes occur during the year without understanding what makes them happen, in other words, the four elements. They are vital, everyday components in your life.

What I want you to do during the few months that you are studying the elements and how they affect your life, is to keep a diary. Write down everything, everything that you can think of. If you think of poetry, write it down. If you think of words that you once heard that describe the different ways and natures of the different elements, write them down.

If you have written them down, you can then remember them. Go back over them and look at how your views have changed over that period. Look at how your views changed from before you did a meditation, to afterwards. All these things are important, because all these things will help you to understand how things around you work, how they govern your life.

The more that you put into those meditations, the more you will get out. If you just sit there and just think, "Oh! I am a bird!" then that is all that you will ever get out of it.

Do not just READ what has been written down, **GO OUT THERE AND DO IT!** Learn from the experience. Otherwise, you could say, " I read that bit! I did the meditations, but I got nothing out of it." And I would say, "Yes, but did you really do the meditations? Did you actually look at what you are doing, at how your life revolved around these things?"

Please, this is not just a book to read and put on the shelf, it is, I HOPE, an experience for you to live. I want you to do and get something out of each of the meditations that are written here.

In the next part of the book, I will ask you to find a special place for you to go to during the seasons of the year. It is important to find a place that you feel comfortable with, a place that you feel something with. Even if it is a tree in the middle of a park, find somewhere of your own. I have been in London and found small, quiet little gardens, havens of nature in the middle of the city bustle. There are different places to find, if you can look for them, you will be able to find them.

I have all too often heard people say, "Well, I live in the centre of London," or, "I live in the centre of this city and there is nowhere for me to meditate." There is Hyde Park. There are other places in the city that you can find, even during your lunch break you may find somewhere. There are many small areas of greenery around in the cities, if you look. I have seen small patches, just on the sides of office blocks, where you can be quiet and meditate for a while.

It does not matter if people look at you, because you are there to do something that you want to do. Be confident in yourself - it is nothing to do with them!

Once you have found your special place, then use it. Keep going back there and use it for the same meditation throughout the year, as I will ask you to do and I hope that you will get as much from doing it as I did when I did it. O.K.? Thank you very much.

The Circle

The circle is the place where you work in the Craft. The idea is to make a place sacred, a place between the gods and the earth, a place that is pure and apart from the mundane world. We have looked at the elements. When you cast a circle, you are asking for those elements to watch over you. I am not going into detail on a circle that is the sort that would be cast by a group, because that is not needed here. What I will explain is a circle for oneself, in other words, a private place, a sacred place.

Take four candles and, if you wish, a statue, or something that means something special to you. Place the candles at four points of the circle, at the north, south, east and west compass points, or quarters as they are usually known in the Craft. Place yourself within them with your statue if wished, and call on each of the elements in turn.

Go to the north and call upon earth, the element traditionally associated with that direction. By this time you know how earth feels. You know how to feel it. So put that feeling into that quarter. Then move to the east and call upon air, ask it to be there, to join with you, so that the place that you are making is sacred to it. Then go to the south and call upon fire. Finally call upon water in the west.

I will not tell you what to say, because these words should come from your heart. To each individual it should be different, so sit and think and maybe write something appropriate based on what you have learnt so far to concentrate your thoughts. It does not matter if you change the words when you actually cast the circle, it is the visualisation and concentration that matter.

When setting the circle up, don't forget that it is a sphere, not a flat circle. Remember the earth beneath your feet and the sky above your head.

When you cast a circle form it in your mind actually mark it out with something that you feel is sacred, using the tip of a knife, or perhaps a wand that you have made. After you have cast the circle in your mind, call upon the earth beneath your feet and the sun above your head to finally make the place sacred. The phrase I usually use is:

"Earth below Sky above Let this circle be cast with love".

Now you have a sacred place.

When you have finished working, you should always close the circle down. Thank each of the four elements in turn and bid them "farewell". Then visualise the circle being dissolved.

The Festivals

Yule

Many people writing about the festivals start with Samhain, but I am starting with Yule because it is still fresh in my mind from the last celebration. I can still see a group of friends gathered in friendship and in love. I see them slowly walking into the living room where the circle has already been pre-cast.

Four people, each taking an element at their respective quarters and each calling it in their own way. A priest and priestess coming together to invoke the God and Goddess. Once that is done, friends are invited into the circle with joy and laughter and the priest leaves. The priestess turns to the people there and starts to explain about Yule, about the Holly King and the Ivy Queen and the battle between the two for the supremacy of the sky and the sun. For if the Holly King wins then he shall reign and if the Ivy Queen wins, her blanket of snow shall last for many more months.

Breaking in on the explanation, the priest comes back bearing a crown of holly and demands the sky back, the Queen turns and refuses, telling him to be gone. The priestess taking her part stands with a crown of ivy upon her head and tries to turn back the usurper saying *"No, no, now is not your time, go leave me"*. The Holly King stands firm and demands entrance once again, she refuses him tardily, saying *"You don't belong here get away with you"*. In response to this the holly king issues the challenge, he brings forward his champion and challenges the queen to a contest for the sky itself. Her champion steps forward and takes up the contest.

At this point everyone goes outside so that the men will have

room to fight, they fight either with swords, staves or sticks. To whichever one wins goes the prize, if the Holly King's champion wins, then the sun returns and the days get longer. If the ivy queen wins, then her cold and darkness stays, the earth does not thaw out yet and everything sleeps on.

After the contest is over, everyone moves back indoors, into the warmth, returning to the circle. They link hands, feeling the warmth of friendship, and dance sunwise to welcome the longer warmer days. After the dancing everyone goes through to a table laden with food and the celebrations begin. Traditionally the Ivy Queen and the Holly King take precedent at the head of the table and the friends and people of the circle sit around them and join in the feast. It is a time of great jollity and merriment and the place is decorated with holly, ivy and mistletoe, the greenery having been brought in during the day. A holly and an ivy wreath is put on the table itself with candles.

Now that we have talked about the celebration itself, here is something for you to do. Find a place you can use throughout the year, to notice the differences and changes in, be it a small part of a wood or heathland, go there and look at how things are. Try to link in with the place, to make contact with it. At this time of year most things will look dead, but you will begin to realise that it is not dead, just sleeping. I want you to feel its energy while it sleeps, the fact that it is drawing itself in, in readiness for the spurt of new growth in the spring of the coming year. Become part of that, meditate with it. It will make it easier for you to notice the differences as everything changes through the year. Find somewhere quiet, where you can be alone, sit down, take a blanket or something comfortable to sit on and start to feel the place. Listen to the birds and animals in it, listen and look, try to use all your senses to completely feel the place. If you can find a tree, go to it and try to feel it breathing, its heartbeat. Feel the rhythm of the place and you will have taken the very first step on a long road.

Now is the time of spring, everything is starting to grow, animals are starting to come together and in your chosen place you will notice the first stirrings of the earth; plants coming out, tree buds starting to burst through. This is a very wonderful time, a time of life, a time when the Lady is restarting her growth. Go to your special place and sit down quietly, the animals might even start to get used to you being there now and show themselves if you are lucky. Sit there and meditate a while, feel the flow of life beginning to move in the earth. Reach out with your mind and your heart and listen to what is there, you will be surprised at the number of noises that are there.

Beltane or May Day

Now we get to May. What happens in May? An awful lot, if you think of how enthusiastically Mayday is celebrated in many parts of Britain; the Maypole, dances, the May Queen and all she represents.

The May Queen represents the earth itself. She had to be chaste, virgin, her sacrifice would have been her virginity in days gone by. I think many people forget about that, or perhaps try to forget about it. A lot of villages have their own particular celebrations, their own traditions that still continue on May Day. In many counties, morris men go to the top of large hills and dance in celebration and bring in may - hawthorn blossom. It is considered unlucky to bring may into the house, but sprays of it can be fixed at doors and windows. Wiccans tend to come together to celebrate May in a different way. All through the night they will have started preparations, singing, dancing, being together.

I'll take you back to that circle of friends, back to that group of people who have come together to celebrate. If you can imagine them winding their way to your special place, to your glade. You can hear them in the distance, singing, laughing,

beating a drum, you see them enter and cast their circle.

Once the circle is cast, the maiden of the group leaves, wearing the cloak she came in. The priestess who is taking the part of the crone places herself in the middle of the circle, with the warrior at her side. The maiden returns, without her cloak, but dressed in green and bright vivid colours, as she comes to the edge of the circle, she does not ask entrance, she just enters. The warrior goes to try to stop her, but she turns to him and says *"How can you stop me entering? How can you stop me coming into your life? For I am spring, I am here, now is my time"*. The warrior backs away. The maiden then approaches the crone, saying *"Why are you here old woman? Now is your time to leave"*. The crone is put out by this and demands what right the maiden has to be there. The maiden explains that she is the May, it has been the time of winter, but it is now her time to come forth and take her place. Gracefully the crone leaves to give way for the maiden of spring to enter the lives of those around her.

In days gone by Beltane was a celebration of fertility, and for many it still is. People would go into the woods and enjoy themselves with their partners. The Beltane child was always looked upon as the blessed one, a gift from the God and Goddess. Great merriment would be had and celebration. If you can imagine the circle after this would sing and dance, light a fire and jump it, the idea being that as you jumped the fire all the bad spirits and negative things leave you. The spirits of the winter and darkness fall away. The ashes from the fire would be spread on the fields to help bless them.

Even today in some places where the farmers still talk with Wiccans, a farmer will go to a witch to bless his fields. I personally know of two farmers who continue to do this, still believing that the priestess who wanders the fields is strong and potent for the land itself. So now we see the spring coming in, in its full glory, we see the buds of the trees and plants opening, we see young birds and animals starting to appear. It is a time of life, of rebirth a time when a sense of life fills you.

Midsummer

A great deal can be said about Midsummer. I want to take you to a time when the sun is warm. At this time of year, it is not just warm, it is really hot. The sun is at the point where the day is at its longest. We start celebrating on the eve before the longest day. Some people stay and have an all night vigil until the dawn. I will describe the most recent one that I went to.

It was at the Rollrights, a place that I dearly love and visit whenever I can. The evening began when I arrived to meet up with friends and the lady who owns the circle and who many look upon as the guardian of the place. We have great love in our hearts for her. We were meeting up with friends, old and new and watching people go through into the circle to do whatever they wanted to do, to connect with it, or just to sit and drink with friends. It is a time when some people dance and celebrate, play instruments, laugh, cry, build fires to welcome the sun in the morning. On this occasion, people came and went, young and old, new-age, old-age, hippies, travellers, just to come and feel the place.

I think the strangest sight of the night, was to see a policeman with a pair of dowsing rods, dowsing the stone circle while somebody held the light for him. It is a sight that I have never seen before and I doubt that I will ever see again.

As the dawn came nearer, people would filter in or go onto the top of the hill, beside the circle to watch the sun rise. Something I always do, is to take some wine and some bread and I just very simply bless them, for the Father and the Mother, for the Sun and the Moon and I hand it round to the people who are there.

Then, as time has passed by and the sun has risen somebody would use a magnifying glass or a lens and take a light from the sun to light a small fire so that they could light a candle or an oil-lamp and that would be kept burning through the day. It would be used, that evening to light the fire again. The celebrations would not happen at night, they would happen during the day, but those times are past. Still, in some out-of-the-way places, people still celebrate Midsummer when the sun is at its highest.

I want to take you back to that stone circle, to the Rollrights, a very old and beautiful place to go, although there are many other marvellous places to visit at Midsummer throughout the country. Some people in this area spend the festival at Avebury, some on White Horse Hill at Uffington, some nearby at Waylands Smithy and some still try to hold it at Stonehenge, but access to that has been forbidden to us. There are signs of this changing so perhaps one day, we may be able to go back and celebrate the rising of the sun there.

What legends are there connected with Midsummer? To me it is the time of the male. It is a time when some groups would dedicate their priests. As the sun rose at Midsummer, the priest would take his vows to the Lord of the Sun that he, himself, represented within the circle. It is a special time, I think, more for men than for women, because it is their time. The time when the Lord overshadows the Earth. It is particularly their day.

I want you, on this day, to find somewhere that is quiet and away from everything. Stop and look around. If you have gone back to your special sacred place, look about you at the plants and the flowers. Some will be in full bloom by now while others will have shed their flowers and started to form fruit or seedheads. The elderflower has shed its blooms and started to show its berries. Fruit is starting to appear everywhere. It is a time, not just of growth, but of the maturing of that growth, where you see the seeds starting to appear on some plants, the fruit and the grain starting to swell with the promise of harvest.

Go back to your place in the woods, or wherever you have chosen and look at how that place has progressed, whether the trees have stopped budding and are starting to show their nuts or fruit, or whatever else you can feel around you. I want you to sit down. Feel the sun on your face, feel its warmth. I want you to start clearing your mind and just thinking about and feeling the warmth of the sun. Think of what that day means. Think of what that time means. Gradually calm yourself down and meditate and naturally communicate with that land that is around you. In doing so, feel the difference and try and remember the difference between now and what it was like at Spring time. Feel and be felt. Remember that feeling is a two way thing between you and the Earth. As you draw yourself out of that meditation, do not forget how that felt. Do not forget what you have seen around you.

Lughnassad

Now in August there is another major festival - Lammas or Lughnassad. It could be said to be a confusing festival since it is celebrated at three different times. Some people celebrate on the eve of the first of August, some on the last day and some when harvesting has begun, when it 'feels' right rather than simply being dictated to by the calender on the wall.

It is a time to celebrate the fact that the fruit which you saw at Midsummer is now starting to ripen and it is the time to begin the collection of that harvest. I usually celebrate when the first bushel of corn is taken in from the local fields, because I feel that that is the time of Harvest. Traditionally, later in the year at the end of harvest, the best of the last sheaf of corn was taken and made into a corn dolly and kept in the house through the winter. Come springtime, that corn dolly would be ploughed back into the Earth. You were taking the best of the Summer, saving it until the spring and re-entering it into the Earth again to re-vitalise it.

This is a time when the fruits and corn are starting to ripen, ready to be gathered over the next few months, between now and Samhain, to be stored for the winter. It is a time, for me, of the beginning of bottling, jam making and generally storing what I can find, to help through the winter months.

I can remember one year when the harvest was very erratic and nobody was quite sure when to celebrate. I sat down and I thought very hard and I looked at the full moon, as it was then. I looked at her, in her fullness and I said My Lady, I do not know the right time to celebrate this year. Please will you give me a sign? Will you give me the sign of three ears of corn given to me? That was her reply, for me to look for three ears of corn, which would be given to me and that would be my sign for celebrating the harvest that year.

I walked into, of all places, a newsagents and I was looking at magazines and then I noticed a woman standing beside me. In her hand were three ears of corn and she turned round to me and said, *"I think you should have these. I do not know why I picked them, but I think that I should give them to you"*. I smiled within myself and thought, Lady how could I ever have thought that you would not answer me? So I took the three ears of corn with some flowers and I took them up to Wayland's Smithy and celebrated with friends. We celebrated the coming of the harvest.

The coming of the harvest is one of those festivals that is usually celebrated by a big feast, with the best of the fruits. It is a sign of the celebration that the Gods would have at that time.

How do you celebrate this wonderful time? Some people like to make a special loaf from the first grains to divide amongst a gathering of friends. Others start a special brewing of beer to celebrate the end of harvest at Samhain later in the year. Beer is also a traditional drink at Lughnassad with some groups. More than anything else, the best idea is to celebrate! Have a meal! Enjoy it! Invite friends round - lots of friends. If you can, have on the table, foods and decorations that you have gathered from your garden or perhaps the hedgerows.

These are all things that would take place during Lughnassad. It really is a time to celebrate the fruits of what is going on around you, not only the fruits of the earth but also consider how your own efforts are coming to fruition in your life.

Again, 'link in', feel yourself into the land. Calm yourself down and feel what has changed there and see what changes have happened in your life and how this time of year has affected your life.

Samhain

The next festival is, I think, probably the most controversial, the most misrepresented by the media and others. In many ways it is one of the most important celebrations for Wiccans and members of the Old Craft because it is our New Year, the day between the old year and the new. Samhain, Hallowe'en or All Hallows Eve, call it what you will, this is the time when the veil between the worlds is at its thinnest and spirits are thought to come out in the night. It is true that the veil between the worlds of the living and the dead is very thin at this time.

We light candles and put them in the window to help spirits who have lost their way find their way home. We welcome those we have loved who have gone before us back into our house and back into our hearts. We remember those who have left us, but it is also a celebration, one of the most raucous and full of merriment apart from Mayday. It is a time when we not only remember the past, but tell fortunes and look into the future.

There are many old folk lores and traditions that go with this time.

This is the night when we light candles to remember those we have loved who are no longer with us. We do not try to draw or force them back, rather we simply remember family and friends who are no longer with us, and, yes, pets too. Remember and leave the invitation open. Look at the candle flame and remember. Think also of all the negative things that have happened over the past year, things you want to leave behind, then, when you are ready, blow the candle out, or if you are celebrating outdoors, let the wind dowse the flame.

This is also the time when we welcome Herne, the leader of the Wild Hunt which can be heard in the storms and gales of the winter months.

Apples are a traditional food at this festival, a sign of the end of the harvest. If you cut through an apple crossways you will see the seed area forms a pentagram - the sign of the cycle of life, death and rebirth.

In one tradition, a young maiden peels an apple, trying to peel the skin all in one piece and then throws it over her shoulder. The initial letter of her husband-to-be's name will appear in that shape.

Some people believe that placing talismans under their pillow will make them dream of the man that they are going to marry. Look into the fire across your shoulder and you will see the face of your future husband. There are so many legends connected with future marriages, in other words, new beginnings.

Let us not forget that although in a way, this is a time of remembering death, it is also a time for celebrating life because it is the New Year. It is the new time coming up. It is a celebration of both, hence, people jump over the fire to purify themselves in the flames. It is a very strong festival. Alas, it has a lot of bad connotations now. Some troublemakers go out on All Hallows Eve to make things difficult for Wiccans to dance and celebrate at major sites. Because of that we have had to find more out-of-the-way places that are less well known. We have had to hide ourselves away which is a shame really because it is a time of great rejoicing and of great merriment.

For this night, rather than going to your special place as on other times, you may like to consider going there earlier in the evening, perhaps before it is fully dark. This is not only because of local witch hunters and the idle curious, but also the spirits are out on this night so it is better to do it during the day. Relax, think into the Earth and feel how the place is different consider how it has changed during that year. Make a note of it and see how you feel the change. That is the most important thing of all. Once you have done that, go back to your home and perhaps do some divining of some nature, with Tarot cards, Runes, or whatever method you prefer. Ask just one question, one question only and see what it draws out - it is meant to be a very good night for doing that sort of work.

Now we have looked at the full cycle of the festivals and a little bit of how the year has gone. Now let us look at the changes that it has brought about in yourself. Do you feel yourself stronger? More knowledgeable about the place? Remember you have seen this place through the full cycle of the year. Now you have seen it when it first started with snow, when the first buds appeared, through to the first flowerings, the starting of the fruit to grow, on to the harvesting time and further on when the land once again goes back into its sleep.

I want you to sit down, at home or in that place and I want you to think about that year - a pathworking of the seasons.

Start off with the snow of winter, damp underfoot, the coldness giving visible form to your breath, he frost on the trees, the sleepiness around you. Take your time. Be gentle. Then go on to the spring time, the first birds starting to make their nests, the first buds, the snows melted and the ground is beginning to live again. Then move on. Now the leaves are on the trees. Now the buds are starting to appear on the flowers and the birds are in full song, having mated for the first time. As you relax, I want you to move on again. Move on to the time when the flowers are now open, full of life. The whole place is Alive with love and laughter. Slowly take the next step, from the sun at its height and the plants in full flower to the time of bearing fruit, when the fruit is all around you and you reach out your hand and touch. Then move on to the time when the trees drop their leaves, when the forest and woodland is green and brown. Then on to the time of the first cold when the trees are bare of leaves, back to the time of sleeping, back to the snows and the storms.

Think about how things have changed. Think about how, during that year, you have changed. Are you the same person that first went to that glade? Have you changed yourself? If you have, do not be scared, it is your real self coming out, the inner self. Many people have commented to me through the years of how they do change, how they begin to find themselves, how they begin to be more sure of themselves. Do not be scared of that, look at it, understand it because that is the inner you coming out. Once you understand fully about the things around you and how and why they are there you understand more about yourself.

I hope that the journey of the seasons, the first part of this, has been a journey for yourself, a journey through that full cycle, a journey through your own mind, a journey of acceptance of what is around you. Now you begin to realise that the energies and the life, even as you walk down the street, are there, in the tree that you may pass on the corner, in a woodland or in a park that you might find in a city. No matter where you go, where there is a green tree beside you, grass under your feet, life is there.

Think about what we are doing to that life as a people, as a race and try and do at least one practical thing about it. If you do only one thing, at least you have done something, made a contribution. As a people, we tend to pay little or no attention to our land. We ignore its inheritance, its life. In times gone by people looked after the land, they respected it. The farmer would ask a local witch to bless his land, to be part of that land. During this time and perhaps in the future it will be that way again. Already, some farmers are turning from pesticides to more organic styles of farming. Perhaps one day they will more fully go over to that way, a more natural and wholesome way and the food producing processes will return to a sustainable non destructive way.

One thing I have particularly noticed over the years is that there are more and more people suffering from allergies and that is partly through what we are eating. Are we eating the right things in our diet? It is all part of learning the natural way of life. The more natural the food that you eat, the more you will feel in harmony with your body, as the saying goes - 'you are what you eat'.

Sometimes for my own health, or for a ritual, I will follow a special diet. First, I will cut meat out of my diet, then the next day, I will take out the pulses, the following day, I will leave out the vegetables, so that I am then down to fruit. Then after the fruit, I spend a day on fruit juices, then on to water, to cleanse the entire body. If you are going into meditation, it is a good thing to do. If you are taking any form of medication or have problems such as diabetes or anything similar, **do not do it**. Talk to your doctor first! I do not want people going into comas, because they have tried to do it and it is not the right thing for their body, because that would be a very foolish thing to do.

There are other ways to do it. You can look at and think about the foods that you can and cannot eat and gradually move on to a more natural and healthy diet, in other words, fewer tinned foods, more natural foods. You will find that this will help to balance your body out and help you be more in touch with what is going on around you.

I know that many of my Wiccan friends are vegetarian, but I am afraid that I will most likely stay a carnivore! For certain times though, for certain work that I do, I will cut out all meat and fish, but I think it is up to the individual to choose that part of their lives.

Affirmation

Now that you have meditated through the elements and through the earth place that you chose for yourself, I want you to consider, "Is this what I want to do with my life? Do I wish to follow the pathway of the Lord and Lady? If so, am I ready to take an oath to swear to the fact that I am ready to follow their pathway?"

If this is the case, there is something that you can do. We call it affirmation. It is not an initiation, because initiation is a process of rebirth, it is a process that you really need to do with other people around you. Although I have heard people say, "I am self initiated," I wonder if they really know what they are talking about because initiation is an experience, it is an experience of rebirth, of being born of the Immortal Mother. During an initiation the priest and priestess enact the roles of the Immortal Father and Mother. Now, as I have said, I do not feel that this is something that you can do for yourself, but I do feel that you can take an affirmation by yourself, in other words, an oath to say, "I will follow your way, Lord and Lady."

If you decide that this is what you want to do, either go to your own personal sacred place, or perhaps to a stone circle or other sacred place. Take with you the things that you feel are important to you in your following of the path. If you have a crystal ball or a pack of Tarot cards that you have used, take those. If you have a chalice that you have used to drink wine from, take that with you. If you have started to bring together the bits and pieces that people use when they practice the Craft, then take those with you as well.

The first thing to do is to purify yourself, in other words, think of yourself underneath flowing water, under a waterfall and think first of all of that waterfall coming up over your head and gradually flowing over your body and washing away any disharmony, anything that you would rather leave behind.

Then think very carefully what you want to say. Remember, this is an oath of love, of love from your heart to the Lord and Lady, to the God and Goddess. It is an oath that only you can make for yourself. No one else can make it for you.

I can remember when I made that first step and I think it went along the lines of, "Lord and Lady, you are my life, you are my soul. You are the Love that I believe in. On this day, I dedicate my life to you, I dedicate my soul to you to follow your pathway and to try and lead my life by your ways of peace and love."

The pathway of the Lord and Lady can be a very difficult one to follow. In this world one can so often come up against the prejudice and hate of people not understanding or respecting your chosen spiritual way. These are things that you will have to contend with throughout your life. It is not in any way easy, but can be immensely enlightening and rewarding. It is a path that in some ways will bring you grief and in other ways will bring you greater joy than you could have found by any other means. It can bring greater peace of mind and greater honesty. If it did not, I would not have followed it all these years.

I am afraid that the word, "witch" still has unfortunate connotations attached to it that have us dressed in black clothes with pointed hats and broomsticks! It is not an image that we are going to lose for many years. I hope that one day, we can hold our rites and rituals out in the sun, out during the day. In fact, during the last few months there has been a growing movement to hold ceremonies such as handfastings during the day. The most recent one I saw was at the Rollrights on Midsummer's Day. I saw a young couple take their vows of love there at dawn, a most moving sight. There were three policemen standing just to one side. None of them laughed, none of them sniggered. They just stood and watched with interest.

The more that people realise that the Wiccan religion is quite normal, is quite peaceful, the more they understand what we are, the less afraid of us they will be. The less afraid of us that they are, the fewer fingers will be pointed at us and the more peaceful will be the life that we are allowed to lead.

One day, I hope, the pagan religion will be a recognised religion in this country. It is one of the oldest, it has it's roots in the earth and the sun. It was here before any of the later importations arrived from the east - it feels right, it belongs here. In some countries the old ways are still a recognised religion - the Norse tradition in Iceland for instance. I understand that the Quakers have already accepted Wicca as a recognised spiritual path so there is real hope for further understanding.

Like any other religion, we have our fundamentalists, though fortunately very few. The Craft is a tolerant religion, seeking to answer questions and understand the path chosen by others rather than evangelise, criticise and mock. As long as people never lose sight of the things that I have tried to explain in this book, there will always be a way forward.

I hope, that during the year that you spend following the things said in this book you would have learnt a lot. You would have learnt about yourself and about that which is around you. If you have followed the way of this writing, then you should have become more of a person yourself. During the bad times, you would have seen yourself, perhaps as others see your worst characteristics, but at other times, you would also see the good points of your life. I hope that this writing has helped to teach you that.

This is only the first step and the first part. The next step contains meditations that are based upon certain places, different sacred places in this country and I hope to take you on a trip through them so that you can enjoy them as much as I do.

May the Lord and Lady always walk with you. May you always follow their pathway and maybe, perhaps, one day, we will meet in love and peace.

Blessed Be.

Sacred Places

This section is about some of the places that I go to worship. It includes meditations that I use when I am visiting those places.

The Rollright Stones

One of the special places is on the border of Oxfordshire and Warwickshire. It is called the Rollright Stones. The legend of the Rollright Stones is that once, the king was going to war and he got to the root of the hill and the local witch turned up and turned him and his people to stone.

Now, the stone circle itself is on the edge of a hill, not quite on the top, but just on the edge.

I have been there during Midwinter and Midsummer. Midsummer, when it has been so busy because there are so many people wanting to do their own thing and Midwinter when there is hardly anybody there at all apart from a few dedicated people.

If you can imagine a small circle of stones, not more than fifteen steps wide by fifteen made up of fairly small stones, only one stone is taller than a man and that is placed at the North. The rest are shoulder height or waist high. They make a full circle. If you sit in the middle, you can overlook the valley itself.

The warmth of a Midsummer's day there, is brought to mind, the birds in the trees can be heard in the background, the calmness, the serenity of the place itself. The stones exude their own calmness. Yet, when people are there doing a ritual, they can be buzzing with life, you can virtually feel them humming.

Now if you should go there, you might meet the person who owns them. She is, to say the least, an extraordinary lady. She is somebody who cares about the stones and the animals around her. She herself, loves the place with a passion. I do hope that you get the chance to meet her one day.

When you go in, go round the stones at first, getting to know them, touch them, feel them. Feel their energy and then walk into the middle and take a seat. Just sit down cross legged. If there are more than one of you, hold hands. Sit in the middle and think for a while. Think about the stones themselves and how they feel. Do they laugh? Can you feel their energy? I want you to gradually reach out your mind to those stones and feel them around you. Think of them, standing there. Just breathe very deeply and very slowly. Relax totally and let the energy flow into you and you will find that they have a feeling too, a feeling that is different, a feeling that is not the same where ever else you go. Try to remember that feeling and take it away with you so that, if you should ever need to feel that way again you can think of the stone circle. Think of the valley and the birds and the trees, if it is winter, with snow crisp on the ground and the love that the place holds. It is a very unusual place. It is a place that I return to again and again.

I will never forget, a few years ago, a group of actors came to the stone circle and they performed Shakespeare's "The Tempest" there. It was a full moon performance at midnight. Prospero stood and gave his speech about magic and as he did, the fog came in until the entire circle was surrounded. It was as though, for that moment, the Gods were there, watching and listening to the performers within the circle itself.

The Rollright circle is a living place, a place that is still used. People go there, actors perform, people go there to see it and to work magic there and to feel the place and it's energies.

Wayland's Smithy

Wayland's smithy is a marvellous place about five miles from where I live. Again, it is on the ridge of a hill. It is an ancient burial mound. The stones at the front are quite large, in fact taller than a man and even if you stretched your arms out you would not be able to stretch right across the width of the stones.

You can actually crawl into the inside of the burial mound. It has its' own warmth and its own feeling. Now, if you can, imagine this burial mound at night, when the moon is high and the magic is in the air. I have been up there and done a ritual when the snow is on the ground and it looks like a sheet of silver. Half way through the ritual a stag came up and stopped to look at what we are doing . After a few minutes he turned, with a toss of his head and left. The place has its own magic.

When you first go there, you will park the car in a parking area and walk along the ridgeway until you get to the site itself. You go along a narrow pathway, between two fields until you reach Wayland's Smithy. There are trees around the outside of it, in an oval shape which form a natural magical barrier. If you stop for a second or two by the small ridge as you go in and say, "Wayland, Lord, may I enter?", you may feel him say yes.

Walk into the actual area itself and then you will find yourself standing in front of the burial mound. It is quite an impressive sight. You can step up to the stone and feel its warmth. It has its own life. If you enter the mound and sit inside it, it feels like a mother's womb, a mother's heartbeat. This is a place, not just of death, but of life as well.

Again, what you need to do is to lose yourself to the place. Feel it, feel it around you, above you and below you. As you look out, you can see the edges of the stones and the trees outside. Feel the place and the energy that is there. Calm you mind and let it and your body relax and see what you see. Do not try to force images, just let the feeling flow. Remember to give back to the place, don't just take. As with so many things in life, the more you give, the more you will receive.

When you come out, think about how you felt. If you have been to one of the other sacred sites that I have mentioned, think about how they compare, how their energies differ, perhaps how they are suited to different rituals or times of year. Come out again into the sun and look at the trees.

As you stand, facing the trees outside, if you are lucky, you might feel the Dryads in the trees. They are there! I have seen many a man sit under a tree with a lost look on his face, not quite sure which way to turn, confused as the Dryads play with them. The spirits are there.

If possible, take up a small flagon of mead or ale and give it to Wayland himself. He always appreciates a good drink! I have actually heard about someone writing a ritual for Wayland and publishing it in a book and forgetting the alcohol! My word, there must be one or two people who go up there to do a ritual who leave a very disappointed Wayland!

The place is a place of its own, of its own making. I have been up there to celebrate handfastings, to initiate people, to take part in rites of passage and to celebrate the festivals. Everything, I think has happened there. Again, it is a place that is alive. It is alive because it is used. Some people go up there to camp overnight, some to do rituals, but everyone respects it.

Now, leave Wayland itself and as you come out, look down to the left and carry on along the ridgeway and walk to White Horse Hill which is only a short distance away.

As you walk the ridgeway you will pass fields on either side of the track. You know, on some winter's night, when the place was covered in snow and, as I said earlier, it looks as if it is just covered with silver. We have looked across those fields and seen a stag, on the top of the hill, as though he is waiting for something, with the moon behind him, silhouetting him. It was a wonderful experience.

Uffington White Horse Hill

On the top of the hill you will find an old hill fort. The hillfort itself is a very special site. It is a place where I have been to have picnics with friends before now, just to celebrate life in general! We have sometimes taken lanterns up there and it is a place where peace is celebrated quite regularly. Pagans from the local area come and circle dance during the Summer. So sometimes you can hear the drums and pipes of pagan music and celebration.

It is a place that I sometimes go to celebrate Midsummer and watch the sunrise. I do not stand inside the hill fort, but just outside, standing above the White Horse itself. The whole place is very magical.

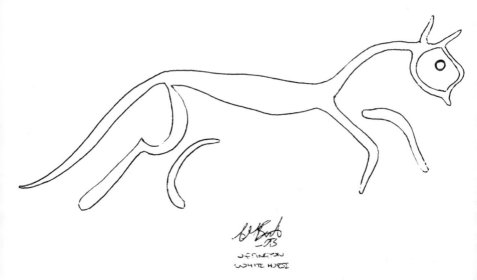

59

They say that if two people stand on the eye of the White Horse and declare their love for each other, that their love will be for ever. Two friends of mine stood on the eye of the White Horse the Midsummer before I handfasted them and pledged their troth. And I am happy to say, that they are still together!

I can remember times when a group of us have gone up on a Midsummer and it has been so quiet up there! Just three or four of us celebrating the fact that the sun was coming up. We were there with mead and bread to celebrate the coming of the sun god. We just quietly stood there.

Dancing, laughing - wonderful. Regrettably the last time that I was there, there were other people who thought it a good place to celebrate but they celebrated with loud music which I did not enjoy, so I left and went to the Savernake forest and celebrated there instead.

First, let us start with the hillfort itself. Sit down and again, I want you to feel the place around you. Feel its life, how it feels. It is a totally different feeling from Wayland's Smithy and from the White Horse itself. Totally different.

When you come out of the hillfort itself, you will look down and see Dragon Hill, a large mound at the base of the hill. Legend says that a dragon's spirit is buried there. It is a place of great earth energy. Again, it is a place where people go and dance. Sometimes, during the summer, you will hear the sound of pagan music coming from there also while people dance their circle dances up there and celebrate life.

It seems that if the government had its way we would not be able to hold rituals at this wonderful place. Some friends of mine actually had an injunction taken out against them by the local police to stop them holding an organised ritual which had been advertised in a pagan magazine. My friends were banned from going to White Horse Hill or Dragon Hill for two months!

Once a year, the local people hold a fair below the White Horse. White Horse Fair has been held for hundreds of years if not thousands. It used to be held on the hill, but is now in a field down in the valley, near to the road. They raise money to look after the White Horse.

The White Horse, of course, represents Epona, the horse Goddess, which is fairly fitting if you think about the valley and what happens there. There are a large number of horse breeders, so there is a very strong connection between horses and the valley. They also say that this horse is the steed for the Wild Hunt and that Herne comes there to fetch her. I have to admit, that once when we were at Wayland's Smithy, we heard a hunt. Hunts are wild. Wayland himself did not want us to leave, we actually felt him telling us not to leave and we did think it rather strange that there would be a hunt out at half past eight, when it was dark. So we stayed and let the wild hunt go by.

Avebury

A few miles to the west of Marlborough is the stone circle of Avebury. This is a place where I have spent many a happy time, I think that I must go there at least once a month.

The stones themselves are set in such a large circle, itself containing a pair of smaller circles, that it encapsulates a village. A part of the village is actually in the middle of the stone circle. They are surrounded by a giant circular mound and ditch. Two curving avenues used to lead into it, though only part of one survives. Modern roads divide it into four quarters. You have the sanctuary, West Kennet Long Barrow and Silbury Hill sites all nearby - a packed area for pagans!

I will start off with Avebury itself. First of all I want you to walk around the complete area which contains the stones walking up on the surrounding ridge. I cannot describe how big

Avebury is, you have to go there and see it yourself. It is the largest stone circle in this country. Many of its stones were destroyed for use as building materials or because they were the "works of the Devil", some still lie buried, but many are standing.

Again, it is a place that is really alive, a place where people go and celebrate. Now that people cannot go to Stonehenge, a lot of them go to Avebury to celebrate Midsummer. As you can imagine, it is a very busy place on that day! You can see people going around and feeling the energies of the stones themselves, going from stone to stone. The church encouraged the village to be built in the circle to lessen the power of the circle, in fact the reverse has happened and the actions of life going on there every day keep the energies alive.

I want you to find a place where you feel comfortable. It might be a coppice of trees, or a stone in the Avenue, the sanctuary, the Cove, or the point where a large stone once stood at the centre of one of the smaller circles or somewhere else around the quarters of the large circle. Just find a place where you feel comfortable and sit there.

I want you to feel the place, to feel its energy, to feel what is there. If you have got a set of dowsing rods of your own, take them with you. See if you can find the energy points in the circle itself. It has a living energy that is totally different from the other sites that you have been to so far. It is a place of earth and water, but also of air - particularly the clumps of beech trees on the surrounding earth bank.

Now, relax and open up your mind to the place around you. You will most probably find that there are a number of other people doing the same thing, leaning against stones, touching them, sitting beside them. Some people go there and stay overnight and sleep under the shadow of a stone. It is a very living place. Once you have finished there, it is time to move on.

If you can, move out along the avenue towards the sanctuary itself. Follow the long line of stones outwards. Feel how the energy differs. Concentrate on experiencing the feeling of leaving, it is something that I often find very difficult. It is as though the place keeps on calling me back.

I took a young man round there a short time ago and he was grinning madly when we came away. He commented that he did not want to leave, he wanted to go back and sure enough, the next day, he did! He did not want to leave even then, because the place feels so very pleasant and comfortable!

When you have gone out of the avenue and found the sanctuary spend a little time there and see how that feels, how it is different.

Then we move off to Silbury hill. No one really knows why Silbury hill has been built. It is large and man made. A lot of women know. A lot of women know that the place is very special to them and groups often congregate there at Midsummer to celebrate their womanhood, because they feel that it is almost a part of them. To many it represents the pregnant womb of the goddess rising from the land. The women go on top of the hill itself and they dance and they sing and they are wild and free!

The hill itself is almost conical shaped, but with a flattened top. The place is so high and steep that it stands out for miles. Much of the surrounding area is flat and you can see it standing there, rigid, growing out of the earth itself.

Once you have visited Silbury Hill, you can walk to West Kennet Long Barrow just a few hundred yards up the road. Now West Kennet has a very strong feeling of its own. You can actually go inside and there are several chambers, with one major chamber. Be very careful if you try to meditate here because a lot of people do a lot of work and the energy is very strong. I have taken people in there who have said that they have started headaches as soon as they entered. That is because the person before has not powered the place down before they have left.

You may find dried flowers in there, offerings left for the Earth Goddess and sometimes there are candles and night lights on stone ledges or the signs of dripping wax.

Half of the barrow has collapsed and parts of the roof are now concrete, but you can enter part of it quite easily and some people stay the night and work magic there. Working parties often have to wait their turn at the major festivals!

It is a place that you can get lost in if you are not careful, where your mind can get lost. Inside, it is dark and damp, but you can "hear" the place and feel the place quite bright with its life. You can feel its heartbeat and feel it slowly drawing its breath in and out. The barrow itself is strange at the best of times. Go there, feel the place, but I would not advise you to meditate there. Meditate above it, but not inside.

I remember taking my circle there once and I was so full of energy when I came out that I embarrassed them totally, because I was as high as a kite! I remember turning around to this poor, poor person, I do not know who they were, who was discussing whether witches used the place and said, "Of course they do! It would be stupid not to. It is a place of life! A place of so much life!" At this point, the people with me got very embarrassed and all went red and shuffled away quickly muttering, "We're not with her!" I could not help it, the place gave me that much energy. Even now, when I think of it, I can feel the way that I felt then, so high, so happy and so free! I felt as though my spirit were free and I had nothing to worry about in this world and as though life was a wonderful thing to live and that the energies which the Mother had given me were part of my life for ever. I regretted leaving the place and I still return so very often to it.

Glastonbury

Now let us move away from the Avebury area, onto another very sacred place. This is an area that has, through the years, regrettably fallen heavily under the influence of commercialism - Glastonbury.

There are two wells at Glastonbury. They are both quite close to each other. One is the White Well and the other is the one that everyone goes to, the Chalice Well.

The Chalice Well garden is a wonderful place to go and relax. If you go in there and follow the pathway up, there is a small pond. Beyond there is a small enclosed area with a waterfall. Basically, the water comes out of the wellhead itself into a small trough and then down to the waterfall. It is a place where a lot of us have made our vows to the Goddess in the past. People put crystals into the waterfall itself to let the flowing water dissipate the energies of the crystals. We have often come across like-minded people there, leading to many an interesting conversation. It is a meeting place of all religions, not just paganism, but Christians go there as well. Glastonbury is a sacred place, not only to pagans, but also to Christians and as such, we should not dismiss their influence there.

The Chalice Well garden is a very good place to meditate. There are seats there, so you can sit down and be quiet. It is a place where you can hear animals around you. I want you to sit there for a while, reach out and feel the different energy. Feel the energy of the water, because this is a place of water. Feel it. Delight in it. Go to it and put your hands into the waterfall and feel the energy from the water, its cool " crispness ", its laughter in a way, as it falls down. Feel it around you.
People used to go there to be healed, hence, at the end of the water fountain you have a place where you can stand in the water. That is what the waters are, in a way, they are a

cleanser, a healer. Many of us take away Glastonbury well water to make our mead and our wine, so that we make it with sacred water. We also take away water to use in rituals. A lot of Glastonbury people, who live near, some of whom are pagan, drink the well water and only the well water because it is fresh and sweet.

If you go up to the well head itself, you can look down into the spring. Even during the droughts, it has never dried up. It has always been flowing, always, never stopped.

Spend a while in the garden, walk around it, feel its serenity. See the blooms of the flowers around you. Spend some time, meditating and feeling the energy of the place, until it is time for you to move on.

Next door to the Chalice Well garden there is a small road. If you go up that road, then on the right hand side, there is a building. In that building is what is called the White Well. The White Well has a different feeling about it. There are some people in the pagan community who run a small tea shop in there and one or two small shops. The water even tastes different, though it tastes just as fresh and again, it is another sacred well of the mother. Just stay there a while and meditate by the well if it is possible and again, feel the energy and how it differs from the chalice well. Feel the water between your fingers.

Glastonbury Tor

Now that you have felt the two wells, I want you to go up to the Tor, up to the top of the hill. This is a place of air, you can feel it building as you walk up the hill. There is also the Glastonbury maze to consider. It is said that if you walk the maze, you walk back in time. I have tried it once and just before we thought that we had got there, someone broke the concentration. The maze takes about three hours to walk.

Walk to the top of the hill. Stretch your arms out and feel the wind. Feel it pulling at you. Take a piece of cloth and feel how strong that wind is. While you are there, if you can, do the wind meditation that I described earlier in this book. It is a wonderful place to do it, but be careful that you do not get blown off or you might find that your "bird" is half a mile away from the Tor! Feel the wind yourself, feel it flowing through your body. This again is very much a place of life. Meditate there a while and feel it around you. Feel the Tor building, there like a stark beacon, standing out, tall, proud. Meditate in there a while and feel the energy of the Tor itself. Feel its life. Feel the air, surrounding, buffeting. Stay there a while and feel its peace.

I have been up there at night and met up with other pagans, who were sitting there, beating their bodhrans, singing and laughing together, as one, united by their love of the place and their love of the gods. I have joined in for a while and sat and laughed and just enjoyed myself.

Tintagel

After leaving Glastonbury, I am going to take you to another place, further down into the West Country, to Tintagel in Cornwall. You go down the hill to Tintagel itself. Now, it is not so much a sacred place, but it is a place of the sea and of the things of the sea. I am mentioning it because it is a place well worth visiting to feel the energy of the sea surrounding it. It will give you a chance to see how the water feels different. If you can get there, please, do go.

Stonehenge

Now, over to Stonehenge. An awful lot has been written about Stonehenge, the place of the Druids, the place of the Sun God. Well, if Stonehenge is the place of the Sun God, then Avebury is the place of the Earth Mother.

Stonehenge has not been treated with love. Stonehenge has been treated with coldness. It has barbed wire surrounding it. People are no longer able to get in there to touch and feel the place, so in many ways, the place is dying. Sacred places need love. They need to feel people around them, to know that they are wanted. Stonehenge was once like that. I can remember it in my youth, before they put up the barbed wire.

Isn't it funny, that the authorities say that Stonehenge will be defaced and yet, if you go to Avebury, where it is completely open, there is no grafitti. Perhaps they should give us back our sacred place. It is going to be a long time before they realise the damage they have done.

When the land containing Stonehenge was given to the nation, one of the conditions was that there should be free public access to the stones. Anyone who has tried to go there believing this in the past few years will have been sadly disappointed!   .

Nowadays, the tourists are shepherded through there and every year we have the same battle to try to get in amongst the Stonehenge stones for Midsummer. They are now allowing a few of us through, a few at a time. That is not enough. Really, all we want, is our sacred place back so that we can go there, dance there, sing, hold marriages, namegivings and make the place alive again.

Stonehenge makes me cry. It makes me cry because of what they have done, but, the place is still in our hearts and as long as it is still in our hearts, then it is alive. As long as people keep on battling to try and reach the place, trying to tell the place that we still love it. Yes, they are allowing us, a few at a time, to enter the circle for Midsummer. They are allowing some of the Druids in, but what about the rest of us? Because pagans are not seen as one group, but as splinters, we are not thought of so highly perhaps. One day, the place will be reclaimed. One day, they will allow us back to what is rightfully ours.

The Nine Maidens

Now I am going to take you to a very small place. It is out on the moors and called the Nine Maidens. It is a very small circle, but it differs greatly from all the others that I have mentioned. It may be small, but it has just the same amount of energy. The stones themselves are not very high, less than a foot, if anything, the largest maybe two feet at the most, but it is a place that is full of life. It reflects the moors and the way that they feel.

It is a place of wildness, a place that you can go to feel the wildness around you. If you can get up there, do try to, but be warned, it is out in the middle of nowhere and the nearest road to it is a mile and a half away and it is very difficult to find. The only reason that I know about it, is that I was asked to do a handfasting there.

I must admit, that the place is absolutely delightful. It has got a different feeling of energy from the other places that I have described. This place is only about ten paces across, not very large at all, but it has got its own energy and its own power and it is a place that is used quite regularly by other Wiccans and by people who are travelling through there, so it is a place that is still very much alive. If you get the chance to, do go there. You will love it! It is recorded in some of the books that you can get on sacred sites and it is well worth trying to find.

This really ends what I want to write about different places that I have been to during the past year or so, different sacred sites that I go to regularly and that I love. What I want you to do when you visit these places is to record what you feel, to write it down, so that you can remember. Also, it helps you to compare notes on how the different places felt, how different their energies were and how they felt to you within yourself. You will be able to see how the meditations differed from each other, but also how they were familiar and very much the same in some aspects. I want you to record what they made you feel, whether they made you happy, sad, laughing, whatever. Then look at your notes and compare the different sacred places that you visit. It is a way of learning, of learning about the energies that are around you, not just the energies that are within you. This is a very important step towards finding the truth within.

The more you go to places like this, the more you will find that you will record. The more that you record, the more you will learn. Never forget to write down, as soon as possible what you noticed, otherwise you may find that you forget things.

The Lifecycle

Our lifecycle goes from birth to death. Let us look at what happens during that period of time. I will look at some of the rituals that we use to celebrate some of the high points of our lives.

The Wiccaning

The first celebration for Wiccan folk is the Wiccanning, when a child is born. The parents, together with a few friends, take the child somewhere where they can see the stars. They show the child to the stars, because, no matter what we do in our lives, the stars are always there. They will always bear witness to everything that we do. As the stars are always there, the Gods are always there, watching and taking care of us.

Then the child is given its name. The parent will call to the Gods, "I name this child ....." and thereafter, that will be the child's given name. Then everyone comes back to celebrate with wine and cake. The baby is given different birthing gifts to celebrate the fact that he/she is now within the family.

Wiccanning is not a commitment on behalf of the child as happens in some religions. It is left for the child to chose her/his own path when older.

Reaching Adulthood

The next stage comes when you are about thirteen or fourteen. Now, I think this is a very good idea, because it actually gives a young person something to go by. I think that an awful lot of the troubles that teenagers go through arise because they do not understand where they are. Are they still children, or are they young adults? Nobody lays the law down and says, 'you are now young adults'. In modern times, we just tend to overlook this. We just say,"Oh, they are acting up". At the age of thirteen or fourteen though, many feel that they are a young adult.

Now the Jewish people celebrate this by the Barmitzvah for the boys with a separate ceremony for the girls. In the Craft, we celebrate it as well. For the boy, it happens at about thirteen or fourteen. It used to be, in centuries gone by, that the boy would be taken out on his first hunt. Up to this point he could have practiced with his bow, but he had never killed with it. He was taken out to hunt his first stag. As a symbol of this, he would be given his first adult bow, with a set of adult arrows. He would be taken off on his first hunt by the men.

We cannot really take a person out for their first hunt anymore, but we can still present them with the bow and the arrows.

What tends to happen, is that the men come together and take the lad into a room that has already been prepared with ale and fruit and cake all ready. They present him with the bow and arrow, explaining that he is now a man and that he has responsibilities, not only to himself, but to the people around him. He should recognise the fact that his peers worry about him and that the adults are here to help him through this stage of life, not just to tell him off! If he has a problem, he should not be afraid of going to them with his problem.

It gives the young man time to think about what is happening in his life. He is no longer a child. He has responsibilities to himself and to other people and therefore he has a clear line to follow, not this hazy sort of area that we have at the moment.

Now, for a girl. It happens when she has her first menstrual period, because up until that point, she is a child. After that point, she is a woman.

The girl is given a crown of flowers to wear. She is taken into the house of the women, or in this case, a room decorated with flowers and different special foods. The crown of flowers is taken from her and she is given a pendant, either of amber or a moonstone. This symbolises the fact that she is now a young woman, that she is now a maiden.

Things are explained to her. She is told that her body is now fertile and she can have children, but her body is also her greatest gift and she should not give that gift foolishly. Men may come, wanting that gift, but it is her right to say no to it. She should only give it in an act of love.

Her responsibilities as a young woman are explained. If there are other children in the house, then it is up to her to help to look after them, to keep an eye on them. What her responsibilities for the rest of her life are is discussed.

It is a real coming of age for her. It marks the transition from girlhood to woman hood.

It is a very special celebration for both boy and girl. I know many pagan children who have gone through the ritual to become adults and they say that at least they know now where they are. They know what is expected of them and if anything, it helps to make them more responsible to themselves and to the people around them, because they realise that they are part of what happens in the family unit, that they are now at an age where they have to be responsible for what they do in their lives.

It is a time when they decide what they want to do with their lives and is a very important transition period.

Handfasting

The next stage, for many, is marriage. We symbolise this with a handfasting. A handfasting is when two people come together with love in their hearts.

A circle is cast. The first thing that is asked if anyone knows if there is any reason why the two people cannot come together as one. If anyone does object, then they have to fight the warrior, who stands on the left hand side of the priestess. I have never seen this happen as yet. Mostly people look at the warrior and think, "No, I do not think that I will bother!"

The next thing that happens is that the couple share a glass, that is a drink of liquid, be it mead or wine, but the vessel is covered over, so nobody can see how full or empty the cup is. At this point they make their vows to each other and to the Lord and Lady.

The next step is that they are bound together using a single cord. This symbolises the fact that they are bound together in the eyes of the Gods and everyone there. The knot can never be broken. They can never be separated. The cord is then cut and given to the bride, with the explanation that although the cords are cut physically, that spiritually, they are never cut and they are bound together always.

The cup is given to the man as a house cup, so each of them have a part of the ritual to keep and take away with them.

In some circles, the couple then run to the woods and consummate the marriage. In other groups an apple is used instead to symbolise the cycle of growth and rebirth. It is cut in half, showing the five pointed star of the seed case, the couple each take a bite, the apple is then bound together and buried.

Then it is time to celebrate the fact that these two people

have come together as one.

Parenthood

Then we have parenthood. I think it is one of the heaviest responsibilities of all. When the first child is born, yes, the circle gather together for the Wiccanning, the naming of the child, but also they gather together to celebrate the fact that two people have taken the first step onto parenthood, which in itself is a celebration.

For a woman, it means that she can now take the place of The Mother in the circle. She is no longer a maiden, but has made her passage to The Mother. The same for the man, he is no longer just the hunter or the warrior, but the father. This is an important step for them both to take in their lives. So their friends come together and celebrate and a lot of food and drink is consumed and there is a lot of merrymaking.

Eldership

The next stage is that of old age. Old age, not just bringing all the aches and pains, but by this time, people have lived their lives, they have learned through pain and through joy. It is a time of wisdom, for many a time of teaching, and a time of relaxing and looking about you. You have lived a life through all the stages by this time and in a way, it is a time to prepare for death.

Death

Now, many people fear death, but a lot of Wiccans do not. They see death simply as the final step of this life, the final step until you start the journey again in your next life. Therefore, there is no fear in death.

When a person dies, we gather together to cut the person's cords. When a person is initiated, they are given cords for life. After they die, their cords are cut, which is a good way of saying goodbye to that person.

The first to be cut is the Earth cord, which is usually cut by the wife or the husband. The air cord is cut by the children. The fire cord is cut by their friends. The last cord is cut by the priest and priestess. It is a very good way of making that final cut with a person, to get the final piece of grief out of your heart, so that you can go on living your life and not always have that person's shadow just over your shoulder.

It is a time for celebrating their life and what they did in their life, how they helped you. Remember the good times and recognise that it is time now for their departure and their sleep.

I have tried to present to you some of the ways that we feel about life and death. Life is the beginning of an adventure. Death is the beginning of another adventure. Through the different stages of our lives, we should learn not to fear death. It is only the final companion.

The Moon and the Sun

The moon and the sun play an important part in our lives. The point of the next two workings is to get to know and to feel their energy.

The Sun

Dawn

The Sun working starts at dawn. You actually have to be up at dawn to see this - not always easy! The aim is to compare three different parts of the day and how they feel and how their energy feels. I am going to describe to you how I see the different parts of the day.

So we start off in the quietness of dawn. It is better to do this in the countryside if you can. The dawn time is quiet, nothing but the birds and the trees and in the distance you can hear the cows waiting to be milked. If in the autumn the mist blankets the ground around you. You can feel its icy tendrils reaching out, but not quite reaching you. Gradually you are aware that the darkness is turning to a twilight, greyness and birds begin to sing their song fully. Perhaps in the distance you can hear the crow of the cockerel waking the farmyard.

You wait and you watch and you listen and gradually you feel the warmth of the sun against your face. Everything around you wakens. The sun forces the mist back, back to the Earth as it gradually heats up and the dew dries. The ground beneath your feet, which is wet, dries out under the rays of the sun. Gradually, he shows his face fully and you can feel the warmth against your skin. The birds sing with heady delight around you, almost seeming to praise the fact that he is there.

I want you to write down how it feels when the sun comes up, how it feels for you. Make a record of it. Do you feel his energy flowing through you? Do you feel at peace or excited? You want to write down these emotions that you feel.

Midday

Then at midday, when the sun is at its highest and everything seems to be still and quiet, almost as though it is waiting for something. The animals around you are busy at work. You can hear the wind rustle in the trees. The wind creates a coolness, so you can stay out in the midday heat. You can feel the heat from him. Be careful! His heat can be great enough to build up and melt the tarmac on the roads. The midday sun is the strongest heat.

Feel him! Does he feel like fire? Does he feel at peace? Put down those feelings again. How do you feel? Do you feel like running around? Do you feel like relaxing? Does his heat make you feel mellow, or excited? Think about it. Think about how he feels.

Sunset

Then, the sunset, when the heat has dissipated. In some places the mist starts to come back and claim the Earth. Everything is winding down. The birds are giving their final burst of song and the animals prepare for the night. You can feel him leaving you, his warmth, leaving the Earth. Gradually, the coldness of the night creeps up as he goes and leaves us.

How does it feel? Lonely? As though you had lost something? As though something that once was there, is no longer there?

Does it feel as though you have lost something and you do not know what? Remember, in the morning, He returns.

At the end of the day, if you are doing this with friends, sit down with them and each of you go through how you feel. Do not be frightened of showing your feelings to the others. Share those feelings. It is part of the growth. It is part of the learning to understand, of being with others. Say whether you felt excited at midday, or quiet and remember to write it down.

The Moon

Moon rise

Now we go on to the moon, the moon in all her silverness, in all her glory. Sometimes as the sun goes down and the moon comes up you can see them both in the sky. The moon, a silhouette and the Sun glowing orange as he dies for the night. As she comes up, you are aware of a different light, as once there was sunlight, now there is moonlight.

What can you hear around you? Can you hear the sounds of the night? Perhaps the owl in a tree? A cricket in the grass?

How does she feel? Do you feel as though you are apprehensive? As though you are waiting for something to happen and you are not sure what? Gradually she rises, until, in her fullness, you can see the silver of her glory.

Feel her. See how She feels. Stand there quietly, listening to what is around you and seeing how things differ around you.

The Moon At Her Height

Then, when the moon is at its height, its pinnacle, how does it feel? Can you feel the energy rising within you? Can you feel the point of energy when everything around you has changed? I want you to sit or stand and to feel how that feeling is. Is it within you, or on the outside? Where is it? Can you find it easily? Is it difficult?

The Moon Sets

Now, the moon sets, it is time for her to leave us. How does it feel? As though there is a loss again? It is a different loss this time. I want you to make a note of how it feels when that Moon goes down. As you see her slowly sink beneath the trees. As you see a lightness where there was once darkness.

Think about it. Think about how the moon shapes our lives, the tides, how things are different. The tide on the full Moon is fuller. Some women's bodies react to the full moon, with the menstrual flow and the flow of energies in their bodies. A pregnant woman might choose to sit and look at the full pregnant moon and meditate. Do you yourself react to the full moon, the moon at Her height? Do you feel different? Do you change at all in the way that you think about things, in the way that you feel? Think about it.

Now that you have finished this, considering the night and the day, look at what you have written. Look at how the two things differ. Perhaps if you do the exercise at different sacred sites, does it differ there? Or at different times of year? Do the things around you feel any different? That is what you are looking for. That is what you are trying to find. All these things are part of you. You are part of them. The more you think and the more you feel, the more you will be ready to take that step to the Goddess.

For, during the day and the night, you have been looking at them both. The Lord Sun during the day and Sister Moon, a part of the Lady at night. It is a very interesting thing to do. If you have to do it alone, then that is the way that it is, but if you can, do it with a group of friends it is far more interesting and you may find, perhaps, that you can explain your feelings easier. Do not feel foolish. It is something that we have all done at different times.

Colours and Tools

Now I am going to look at colours and tools, the things that we use in the Craft and why we use them.

Athames

The first two things are the athames, the sacred blades. We usually have two, one a black handled knife and one a white. Why the two? Well, the idea is that the white handled knife is the one that you use to make things, be it to cut a tree or to make a set of runes, but you use that knife to make things.

The black handled knife is the magical blade - an extension of yourself. You will find that it will store energy and power within the blade. It is used to cast a circle or do other work and you will find that the energy will be built up and stored within the blade.

Cords

I will discuss the cords that we sometimes use in Craft, though not all circles use them. I only tend to use one and that is the brown cord. The brown cord symbolises the Earth. It is six metres long so that a large circle can be made. It can be used to measure out the circle and it is also a symbol of Mother Earth herself.

The other cords that are used by some of the others are the white cord, the red and the blue. The red symbolises fire, the blue, water and the white air. These are sometimes used in what is called cord magic, which is where you make knots in the cords, you loop them and you use them to build up the feeling of magic, the feeling of energy.

Cord magic can be done on your own, or with a partner with each of you taking one end of the cord. The power and intent can be built up by each of you saying a short phrase in turn then tying a knot in the cord to emphasise it and confirm it in your mind.

Chalice

The next thing is the chalice, vessel of the Mother. Some people make their own. Others buy them. If you have skills in that direction make your own whenever possible, even if it means going along to pottery classes. A chalice does not have to be a beautiful thing, it has to be a thing which means something, a thing with feeling, a thing with love.

A lot of the Craft things that I use have been given to me as gifts over the years, but my chalice I found at Southampton show when I was least expecting it. A potter had made it, but it was not, in their eyes perfection, so they were letting it go at a far lower price. To me, it was perfect, with the blue of water, the browns of earth, the white of air and just a hint of red for fire in there. It was a thing that had been made by fire, earth, water and air and therefore it became very special to me. It still is. I use it whenever I do magic.

Wands

The next things are the wands. The wands can be made of glass, crystal or of wood. I tend to use a set of wooden wands, that is, one of oak, one of ash, one of thorn and one of willow.

When I got my wands, I went to each tree and asked if I could take something from them. In return I gave something of myself, either spiritually, or an offering of blood. It may horrify some people out there that I would give a little prick of blood to a tree, but you are taking part of its life, part of itself, away with you. Is it not only right to leave a part of you behind?

The Robes

Now you have your wands, your chalice, your cords and your athames. The next things are the robes. Now a lot of people think that the robes are a lot of hunkum bunkum. The reason why we tend to wear robes is that it can be somewhat cold outside even in the British summer. It feels better to wear something special for rites rather than the ordinary clothes you wear every day.

Whenever possible try to make sure that your robes are made from natural fibres, such as cotton and wool, or at least have a good proportion of them. There is a good reason for this. In a ritual you can build up a lot of static electricity and your clothing will cling to you. Natural fibres also breathe more easily and are less flammable than nylon etc. They also feel better!

There are those in the Craft who say that you should go skyclad, but I cannot see how you can concentrate on a ritual properly if you are freezing cold. A lot of the places that I work at you would get freezing cold. Stand on the top of White Horse Hill naked? No thank you! So therefore, we tend to wear robes.

I myself, wear a good cotton undertunic and a long Celtic style overtunic made from wool, a good warm cloak and a good sturdy pair of boots!

Sometimes I will wear boots to get to a place that I am going to work and then take them off, but there is nothing worse than half way through a ritual to find that you have just stood on a thistle! It really does make your concentration waver! Also, I am afraid that sometimes humans are not so nice to the Earth, so sometimes you find things like broken glass and other things like that out there. I have seen some very nasty foot injuries where people have gone bare foot and found glass. All you have to do is wear a simple pair of sandals if you do not want to wear boots. If I am not wearing boots then I wear a roman style sandal.

What colours should one choose for robes? Good earthy colours, greens, browns; colours that reflect nature itself.

Now that I have quickly looked at some of the items that we use in the Craft, I have to say that a lot of the things used in my own circle have tended to be quite old. Some of the athames for instance have been handed down in the Craft from old practitioner to young. A tool does not have to be old, but it must feel right to you.

You do not just gather your equipment overnight. It can take years, because it takes years to find the right thing, the thing that you feel comfortable with. The thing that you want to use again and again.

Making A Robe

I am going to give a very simple guide to making a very straightforward full length tunic. It is useful to use if you are doing indoor work, having a bath or just want a general change of clothing. With the right music and incense, it will help you to get into the right mood to do the work. A fresh robe, one that you keep only for Craft work will help with that.

The amount of material that you need is from your shoulder height to the floor, about three metres of material. If you can, try to get sixty inches wide material, which will reach from wrist to wrist, so that you can fold the material in half lengthways to give you the long body of the material falling down. All you need to do is to cut a simple tee shape in that material, allowing for your arms and your body. Check the width of your body between the arms. Make a head hole. Sew up the sides. You then have a very simple robe that has not taken that long to make. Whenever possible use natural fibres such as pure cotton, otherwise, if you use nylon, you will have a terrible time with static electricity when you are working. You may have sparks flying all over the place and sometimes that can be pretty painful!

Crystals And Stones

During the last ten years, we have seen a large growth in the occult as an industry and in the use of crystals. We see crystal healing and crystal technology in general, yet it is something that is not new. The uses that the crystals are being put to is very old.

We have not tended to use things like amethyst though, what we tended to do is use stones that we found in special places, be it on the top of a hill or by a fast flowing river or in a place that we find special. It may just be a well worn piece of flint or a stone with a hole in it.

Traditionally, the idea of empowerment into an item such as a stone, is so that the power is released gradually for the good of a person.

If you were doing some healing, you would take your stone, you would then keep it close to you for a couple of days, in your bag, pocket or whatever until you decided that the time was right. Then you would take the stone and empower it with the thought of healing. You might sit down and work inside, listening to some suitable music, or you might choose to work outside underneath a full moon. Gradually put your energy into the stone and the thought of healing, don't force it, just let it flow.

The idea is to then give the stone to the person you are trying to help, so that it gradually releases the energy that you had put into the stone and passes it to the person. Instead of giving healing by touch, you have used the stone to do that for you. You might not be able to be with a person who is at the other end of the country, it might take three or four hours to reach them, but the stone could be with them instead. They are far less obvious than having lumps of raw crystal around the place.

There are many kinds of stone that can be found in this country. Flint is one example which is very common in this area. When people think of flint, they just think of black stone surrounded by white, but I have seen flint with red and orange in it, amongst other colours and they can be just as beautiful as foreign and expensive stones such as a lump of smoky quartz from Brazil. Not only is flint beautiful to look at, but it has a life of its own and strong associations with safety and protection - Think of the exquisite arrow and axe heads made here long ago and of course flint can be used for building and to strike fire for warmth, cooking and protection.

I think that the problem that we have to redress with the crystal industry in general is the amount of damage that it is now doing to some of these countries abroad. The amount of crystal being removed by strip mining is becoming quite ridiculous. Do not forget, crystals are not just sold in this country - every New Age shop carries crystal here, as do their counterparts in America and across Europe.

These crystals have to come from somewhere and we are not thinking about the terrible damage that is being caused to the environment and we are not checking the origins of the crystals that we are buying.

I do have crystals in the house, but most of them are from geology shops and are geological specimens, therefore they are not strip mined, or they are from antique shops where the crystals are twenty or thirty years old.

I try whenever I do buy crystals, to find out that they have come from a source that has not harmed the environment.

Other Uses For Crystals, Pebbles And Stones

One thing that I use stones for is if I have a headache. I do not really like taking medication for them. I tend to focus the pain and put it into a stone and then put the stone into a river. The idea is that the river will wash away the pain and cleanse the stone of the negative energy that I have put into it.

The same process can be used if you are feeling depressed, or on any occasion when you feel that you are surrounded by negative energy. If you sit with that stone and try to put that negative energy into it, then as I said, put it into a river. The energy will then dissipate, it will be washed away and cleansed. If you can't find a river then use the tap, but natural water is best.

I have mentioned the use of stones for healing and using them as tokens for healing. There is no reason why you cannot put positive energy into them and use them as some people use crystals to store energy and power them up for Craft work. You can quite easily use your pebble or stone the same way.

If you are doing some work, have that stone in the vicinity of where you are working and it will soak up any excess energy from what you are doing. If you are doing something to help someone, it will absorb the residual energy of what you are putting out. At the end of the day, the stone will absorb all the natural energy from what you are doing, none will be lost and wasted.

I think that many people tend to go over the top on crystals. There are some houses that have them now all over the place. Why do that when you could have a multitude of stones that hold memories? A friend of mine went on holiday a short while ago and brought back normal beach pebbles and gave them to her friends, but she took them from a place where she felt something special was there, that there was life. The people that she gave the pebbles to agreed. They could feel the life of the place that they came from.

If you are visiting a place, you can take some of the energy of that place with you by taking a small pebble. When you hold that small pebble in your hand at home, it can help bring back and concentrate your memory of the place that you have been to and what you felt in that place. Rather than having a photograph of yourself at, for instance, The Rollright Stones, you can sit and feel again what you felt when you were standing in that sacred place.

The one thing that you should never do is to try and chip pieces off from the standing stones at sacred sites, from sacred stones and circles. Now some of you may be feeling shocked and say, "Oh no! I would never do that in a million years!", but I have actually seen people try to do it! I have been very distressed and gone up to them and said, "Please do not do that!" and explained the reason why and they have, thank goodness, stopped.

I myself have what I call a house rock which I have empowered to help protect my own house, so rather than having a lump of crystal sitting in the living room, we have a very nice stone sitting there instead. That helps to divert any negative energies that are pointed towards me at any time. Occasionally, I take it to a sacred site, a sacred water site such as a sacred well or a river and I cleanse the stone in the river and bring it back to the house and recharge it up for its particular use.

Another point is that stones are not always as obvious as a crystal. A friend of mine has a lovely rock garden in the front of their garden. In amongst the rocks in the rock garden are one or two rocks that she has charged up to help protect her and to protect the house that she lives in. Nobody would know that they are there. They just think it is a very nice looking rock garden. If you put one or two crystals in there, they would stand out a mile.

I think that the main message that I am trying to get across, is that it is not necessary to use a piece of crystal that you are going to pay between five and ten pounds for, when you can find a stone that can mean as much and even more, because you have been to the place that it came from. The place means something to you and it brings back a very good memory for you as well as serving a useful purpose. There is nothing wrong with doing that.

Incenses, Their Use & Making

Incenses are, in a way, an older form of the modern aromatherapy. Many of the ingredients that we use will bring about the same effects. Before starting you have to think what you are going to use your incense for. Is it to calm you down before a ritual? Do you want to use it during a ritual and if so, what is the result that you are seeking? Is it to relieve a bad headache?

There are many ways of creating your own collection of ingredients. One way is to go out and collect your ingredients from what is out there, in the wild and in the garden, things like pine resin from the trees themselves. During the autumn months, pine trees release resin as a way of protecting areas of damage during the winter. You can collect some of that resin, but be careful not to damage the tree. It usually does produce an excess of gum.

There are many different kinds of moss and wild plants, but you have to be very careful about collecting wild plants because more and more are becoming endangered species. There are laws in this country which state that you are not allowed to collect some species of plant.

The second method is to grow your own, be it rosemary, camomile, a wide range of herbs and other plants, marigold and rose petals, the sort of plant that you can grow in your back garden. Many herbs and plants have medical as well as culinary uses. I have been at a place before now where I have needed to make some incense and have had nothing on me and so we made what we called a "kitchen incense"! We used all the sweet smelling herbs that a friend of mine had in her kitchen to use for cooking. We also used a mixture of petals that she had for pot pourri. The incense turned out very nice!

The third way is to buy your incense ingredients from places like Neal's Yard in London who do a wonderful selection of dry ingredients. They sell things like dried mistletoe and dried frankincense and myrrh so you can get the gum resins there. There are other specialist shops which supply dried incense ingredients.

You need charcoal to burn your incense on. You can buy this from occult shops, but I tend to go to church shops and buy it there because it is a lot cheaper. I buy it by the box!

To make your own incense mixture you take your dry ingredients, such a mixture of frankincense, any number of herbs and a base oil to mix. If you want to you can also add a few drops of essential oil to your base oil which you use to bind all the ingredients together.

The main way that I make my own incense is to get the ingredients that I am going to use and to pound them down in a pestle and mortar until they form a fine powder if possible and then add a very small amount of oil to bind it together or just coat the ingredients that I have chosen.

I have found that different incenses effect different people in different ways. There are some plants that will set one friend of mine totally on edge and yet it will totally relax another friend.

I have mentioned using different mixtures for different things, for headaches and stress relief for instance.

Insect Repelling For Outdoor Use

Here is a highly practical incense that I often use for an outside ritual:

lemon balm
basil
bergamot
cedar wood (if I can get hold of it)
lavender

Grind these up together. These are all scents which are meant to keep insects away, which in high summer can be extremely useful if you are working outside.

Here are some other ones which I find useful in day to day working.

Headache

If I have a headache I tend to put together a mixture of:

lavender
sweet marjoram
rosemary
violet
cumin

To some it may smell absolutely terrible, but I like the scent once mixed.

Migraine

One that I find very useful; for a friend of mine, that I make up for his migraines is,

Sweet Marjoram
Sage
Yarrow
Basil
Lavender

I tend to make that up for him quite a bit!

Relaxation

When I want something to help relieve stress and to help me relax before I am working, I find the following useful,

lemon grass
scotch pine (collected from a local pine wood)
rosewood
rosemary
ylang ylang (which I to get in oil form)
cedarwood
myrrh

Now those pounded together give me a mixture which I burn before I am due to work to help me relax and I find that it does help.

Those are one or two ideas and recipes that I have used myself in making incense.

What you must remember when you are working is that you are not just using one sense, but all of your senses. You are using your eyes and your ears and also your sense of smell. I think that smell is a very important sense, because that, combined with music can help you to relax before a ritual and help to keep you relaxed during a ritual.

It is something that is important and there are incenses that you can get for different occasions, but the best suggestion that I have is to test things out and see what you feel good with. Try different herbs, different plants and see what sort of things you enjoy.

If you have got no idea of stockists whatsoever, then as I mentioned, I tend to go to Neal's Yard who are very good. I also go to Star Child in Glastonbury. Again, they have a very good selection of dried plants and oils. For straight oils I go to Culpeppers who sell oils for aromatherapy. Those are the three main suppliers that I usually go to. Other than that, I take things from the back garden or I go out and see what I can find in the countryside.

As with anything to do with the use of herbs in this way, you must be careful of the amounts that you use. I have tried to give you some safe ones that I enjoy using and that other people enjoy using, but the main thing is experimentation. What one person enjoys, another person may find irritating and not enjoy.

Regarding incense holders to put your charcoal in, I find that places like Oxfam sell them, in addition to many New Age shops. The basic things that you need are, your incense burner, your charcoal and your ingredients. Do not go out with the idea of buying everything that you need in one go. That would cost you an awful lot of money. Buy gradually, or start growing the herbs that you need and slowly build up a stock of the essential oils that you need.

The incense box that I use, contains I think, about £300 to £400 worth of oils and incense ingredients at the moment. I have just restocked and I bought just a handful of items, a mixture of oils and herbs and that is another thirty or forty pounds added to the cost! The idea is to build up your collection over a number of years. Find a box to keep them in, otherwise the herbs will start to deteriorate and to lose their scent. It helps to keep them all together in one place.

A pestle and mortar is good for grinding and mixing materials. The type that you want is a pottery one. Do not add your oils when they are in the mortar otherwise you will taint the pestle and mortar when the oil soaks into the clay. A better idea is to grind up the dry ingredients and then transfer them into another container, perhaps a small metal one and add the oils at that stage. Then you can put your incense into a jar if you are going to keep it, or, if you have just made enough for that occasion, you will use then what you have made.

Another use for essential oils is, before you begin a ritual or a working that you are planning, first have a bath and think about your day to day activities and then think about the water washing all those everyday things away so that it will put you in a better mind for what you are about to do. If you put a few drops of essential oil in the bath, the scent will help you to relax while you are in the bath. One or two oils that are good for that purpose, to help you relax and feel good are rose, camomile, frankincense, if you can find it in oil form, marjoram, mint, pine. I rather like the smell of cedar wood, ylang ylang, rosewood and rosemary. There are some of the scents that I can think of that will help you to unwind and wind down and relax before whatever it is that you want to do. (Note. One does not usually use more than three essential oils at once, with a total of six drops in a bath. Pregnant ladies, take further advice.)

Divination

There are many ways of seeing into the future. There is the Tarot, the runes, use of a crystal ball, the candle flame, the use of a magic mirror. These are but a few of the methods used for divination. I am not going to discuss Tarot and runes because there are many books about those forms of divination. What I am going to look at is the natural forms of seeing into the future.

I will start with one that I use a lot and that is the use of a candle. You need to get into a state of relaxation, perhaps put on a piece of music that you like and burn some incense. Then darken the lights in the room so that all you have is the candle. It is useful to have a pen and paper beside you so you can record any answers that you receive.

Start off completely relaxed and allow yourself to become totally absorbed in the candle flame. Then think of a question that you want to ask. What you are looking for is not pictures or images, but thoughts. Thoughts will gradually come into your mind and you write down those thoughts. If you are working with someone else then they can ask the questions and you can tell them what you feel and see. I do not mean here seeing an image, but "seeing" a thought in your mind.

If you are answering something for them, try not to think about what you know about that person, but what you seem to know by looking into the flame. It might contradict what you already know about the person, but that is not the point of the exercise. Do not be frightened by what you see. The whole idea is not to let your everyday thinking interrupt what you are doing. Mention exactly what you see in that flame.

The same method is used when you are using a crystal ball and again when you are using a magic mirror. If you are using a magic mirror, it could be a piece of glass that has been smoked over. One magic mirror that we made here was to get a round piece of glass and to burn oak so that we had oak charcoal. We crushed down the oak charcoal, mixed it with varnish and painted it in layers on the back of the glass. We ended up with a complete black surface, when we turned it round after it had dried. It may be grainy and gritty on the back because of the colour that has come out of the charcoal into the varnish, but if anything that will add character to the mirror itself. We made the one that we did over a full moon and we cleansed the glass beforehand in a sacred stream.

You use that in the same way as the candle flame. You might like to work with a candle placed behind you, so that you look into the darkness of the mirror and lose yourself into it. Do not be worried if you do not manage it the first time, like anything, it is a skill that must be learned. Skills only come with time.

Another method, which may seem rather bizarre, but it is a method which we use, is cloud watching. I expect you have lain on your back sometime and watched clouds go by and said, "That one looks like a bird! That one looks like a house!" It is the same sort of thing. You see patterns in the cloud and you read the patterns that you see and interpret them in the same sort of way as you see them.

Another method is that of the old tea leaves. Now tea leaves tends to be an art that is dying out. It is not used so often now as it used to be. I think one reason is the invention of the teabag! Lately though, I have heard of an enterprising person who is reading coffee grinds! I must admit, it is not something I have seen, but I have heard of it, so it must be happening somewhere!

Another form is using the old fashioned playing card. The

playing cards were used as a form of divination before the Tarot cards became so popular. The Tarot packs now are derived from tarrochi cards, used to play a game long ago. The earliest record I have found of a tarochi pack being used for divination is about 1735. The card game itself goes back to the Medieval period.

When we look at modern cards, we realise that tarot packs were the ancestors of our modern playing cards. There are a lot of people who still use an ordinary pack of cards for fortune telling, which is something that I myself do quite regularly.

I have described some of the methods that I use, there are many more and as time goes on, you will come across them in your own way.

The Future Of The Craft

What is the future? Where does the future of the Craft lie? In this country, the Craft is quite strong in its many forms, be it the Old Craft, which is what I follow, the Gardnerians or Alexandrians, whatever. It is growing. We are seeing a youth that is interested, not just because it is an unusual religion, a form of rebellion, but because they feel in their hearts that it is the religion that they wish to follow.

I hope that this book has helped you to have a greater understanding, because the Old Craft is about what is around you and within you. It is not about the fine trappings and the words that are written down, but about the feelings, the feelings of love and the feelings of understanding, of working with the people around you and for the people around you.

It is a pathway that is difficult, it is not easy. If I said it were, I would be lying. There are times when you will want to give up. There are times when you will think, why am I doing this? Am I stupid? Am I a fool?

But then you will find occasions that make everything right, perhaps the time that you see a deer against the full moon or a time when a fox comes up to you because they feel that you are not a danger to them. These are the occasions that make it all special and make it all worth while working for.

You may wonder what is the next step? Well, normally, yes, it is initiation. But I am afraid that there are things that I cannot write down in this book. There are things that are taught by word of mouth only, from teacher to pupil.

I do hope that you will find a teacher after reading this book.

If you are meant to, you will find the right person.

There are many more things that could be said, but putting them into words is difficult. The advice that I have given thus far is the best that I can give.

Go out and feel what is around you. Become part of Nature and by becoming part of nature, understanding Nature, you take the first major step onto the natural pathway.

We are different in the way that we respect the Earth, that we work with the Earth and for the Earth. We are not interested in whether this person knows more than that person. What we are interested in is the wisdom that the person holds within them, be they young or old, the feelings that they have for the place around them.

You can look into the eyes of a person who follows the Old Way and you know that they do. You can feel that mutual feeling of love for the Earth and that which surrounds them. It makes that person stand out from the crowd. You know in your heart that you can reach out to that person and say hello and get on with them instantly.

The time I met the two people who are publishing this book was one such occasion. I was up at Wayland's Smithy with some friends, having a picnic at Lughnassad. We had just finished eating and discussing Wayland himself when a large group of French students came in. We were watching them and listening to them, watching them climbing over the place - they did not really know why the place was there.

Then I noticed two people come into the site with a baby and I recognised them for what they were, by the fact that they had the Craft spirit within. I could see them and I could feel myself about to take a step towards them and say hello, but they went all the way around the Smithy and came back and I knew what they were and I took the step and I said hello and it is a step I have never regretted taking because they are two very close friends of mine.

So when you see that person, do not be afraid, they can only say no and if someone says no to you, there is no reason to be stupid or to feel stupid. It just means, perhaps, that it is within them but they have not said yes to it yet.

There are an awful lot of people out there who are destined to be your friends through the Craft, friends that you have not met yet and one day, you never know, you might meet me! If you do, do not be frightened of saying hello, because I am like everybody else in this world, I have a belief and love. My belief and love is for that which is around me, the stars in the sky, the trees in a breeze and the sacred places that I go to and love so well.

I have tried to share my feelings with you and I hope it comes across to you what I feel about my pathway. Every day I wake up and know that it is a day that I can learn something. It is a day with a beginning, when something exciting might happen. Every day, I serve my Lord and my Lady, with my heart.

Recipes

Here are some traditional recipes for food and drink - important parts of any festival or celebration.

Honey Cake

Honey cake has been used as a traditional festival cake for a very long time. It only has a few ingredients, honey, flour, butter and eggs.

You want:

1 lb of honey
3/4 lb of flour
2 eggs
1/4 lb of butter

You melt the honey and the butter together. Once they are melted, you add them to the flour. Mix it well in and then break in either one or two eggs. The cake should be at a dropping consistency. You then put it into a seven inch square loaf tin and put it in a medium oven for about an hour.

I have found this cake to be popular, not just amongst the Craft, but also with non Craft friends. It is something that is served a great deal in my house. People seem to enjoy it and always come back for seconds, sometimes several times!

Saffron Cake

My next recipe is for saffron cake. It was something that I used to make a lot of and I did not think that it was made anywhere else, except among Craft people. Then I went down to Cornwall and discovered that they have been making saffron cake for centuries. I think it is another one of those recipes that have always been around, but due to people moving away from the countryside, it gets forgotten.

You need:

a pinch or 1/4 teaspoon of saffron strands
1/2 pint of warm milk
1/4 oz of fresh yeast
2 1/4 oz castor sugar
1 lb of flour
6 oz butter
4 oz carrots
2 oz chopped peel

First of all, you pour the milk over the saffron to get the colour out of the saffron. You need to leave it to infuse for about 3/4 of an hour. Then you want to strain it and reheat the liquid to lukewarm.

Next cream the yeast and the sugar and leave it until it bubbles. Then, gradually, very slowly, because you do not want to kill the yeast off, you add the warmed saffron milk. Sift the flour into a mixing bowl and rub in the butter. Make a well in the middle and pour in your yeast liquid. Now leave that to stand in a warm place for about fifteen to twenty minutes until it starts to froth up. You then add the carrots, the mixed peel and any remaining sugar. Mix it into a dough so that you have what is virtually a bread dough. Cover it and leave it in a warm place to rise until it has doubled in size.

Turn the mixture out and then knock it back as you would a normal loaf of bread. (This means to take it out of the tin and rework it, or knock it about some more.) Only work it lightly though, you do not want to give it a heavy kneading. Then you want to shape it into something that will fit about a one pound loaf tin or an 8 inch cake tin. Grease the tin well and cook it in a moderately hot oven, that will be about 180 C for about an hour.

Once you have done that, turn the heat down a little bit and leave it to cool. Continue cooking at the lower heat until the top is a nice golden colour and firm to the touch. Leave it to cool in the tin for a while before you turn it out.

Seasonal Breads

Another traditional recipe is to use a traditional bread recipe and then to add different ingredients according to the season that we are celebrating.

If it is autumn, we would add things like chopped nuts and spices, so that you get a nutty, spicy flavour.

During the summer, we would add bits of apple to a bread dough. This may sound unusual, but it is in fact, very nice. You end up with this nice fresh bread with moist pieces of apple in it.

During the winter months, we make a very spicy bread so that you have currants, apples and spices all in the bread mixture.

These are served during ritual periods, in other words, if you are having a celebration, they are used as celebratory breads.

Yule Pie

The next recipe is what I know as eel pie, though it has absolutely no eel content. You want to get hold of a recipe for a hot water pastry or a short crust pastry, or you can cheat and buy a ready made packet. Now the amount of meat to go inside this should be enough to make a one pound hand raised pie or an eight inch, normal short crust pie.

What you need for this is:

2 chicken breasts, very finely chopped
The bones from a cooked chicken
1/2 teaspoon of saffron
4 oz of sultanas
8 oz of very finely chopped boiled ham
mixed spice to taste
honey to glaze

Boil the ham and the chicken and set aside the stock. Continue to boil the stock in order to reduce it to a jelly. Finely dice the ham with some mixed spice and set it to one side. Add a little bit of water to the saffron to get the colour out of it. Let it steep in boiling hot water for about half an hour. Once you have got the colour out of the saffron, add it to the diced chicken. You also add the sultanas to the chicken.

You take your prepared pie dish, with the pastry already in it if it is a conventional pie. If it is a hand raised pie, then you have it already moulded, ready to put the meat into.

The bottom layer has to be the chopped ham. It is a symbol of the Earth. On top of that you place the saffron dyed chicken. You then take the jelly that you have made and pour that into the pie. It will keep the pie moist. You want to put about five or six tablespoons of the liquid in at this stage. You keep the rest of the liquid back. Put the tops onto the pies and put them into a medium oven. Follow normal pie directions, the sort that you would be given for a steak and kidney pie or for a hand raised pie. Half way through, take some honey and mix it with your reduced stock and use that to glaze the pie. Pour it onto the top of the pie so that it forms quite a thick glaze. This will sweeten the pie, in addition to glazing it.

The symbolism of this pie is quite a nice one. For a Yule pie, it symbolises the Sun's supremacy over the Earth. It is a very nice tasting pie as well!

Vegetarian Yule Pie

Since, in these times, so many pagans choose to be vegetarian, I have included a non meat version of the Midwinter pie, whilst retaining the colour and symbolism.

For the base, representing the earth, take about four ounces of chick peas and soak those overnight. Next day add fried onions to the chick peas and some herbs to make the bottom part of the pie.

For the upper part, representing the Sun, take four ounces of orange lentils and soak them in vegetable stock overnight. Next day mix them with some chopped onions and some more vegetable stock.

Both the chick pea and lentil mixtures obviously need cooking before putting them together for the pie.

When both mixtures are cooked, mix the saffron and the lentil mixture together with a little honey, to make the top part of the pie and place it on top of the other mixture to simulate the Sun being over the Earth.

Yule Pudding

Another wonderful recipe that would traditionally be served at a Yule celebration, would be a Yule pudding. It is really a pagan version of the Christmas pudding, but it is not so dark and is a lot spicier. It is a suet sponge pudding, but with lots of raisins and lots of spices.

You want:

6 oz plain flour with a teaspoon of baking powder or
6 oz self raising flour

3 oz breadcrumbs
A level teaspoon of baking powder
1/4 teaspoon of salt
3 oz suet
8 tablespoons of milk
4 oz raisins
4 oz currants
1 1/2 teaspoons of allspice

Mix the suet, flour, dried fruit and other dried ingredients together. When they are thoroughly mixed, stir the liquid in gradually until you have a pudding.

Put the mixture into a one pound pudding basin which you have lined with greaseproof paper. Steam it for about one and a half to two hours.

Once it is cooked, you turn it out on to a plate and it makes a very nice, light, spicy pudding.

Cider Cake With Honey Icing

Again, this is a recipe which I thought was pretty original until I went down to Cornwall and found that it is still known there. It is cider cake with honey icing.

You will need:

10 oz self raising flour
1 teaspoon of ginger
5 oz butter
4 oz castor sugar
1 tablespoon of honey
6 fluid oz sweet cider

Sift the flour and ginger. Then cream the butter and sugar and honey separately in another bowl. Beat the egg, also separately and add alternatively with the flour to the creamed mixture. Then add the cider, stirring well. Pour it into a greased, lined cake tin, preferably seven inch and bake for at least one and a half hours on gas mark three, which is about 170 C. Then test it before taking it out.

Honey Icing

I use this with a lot of cakes, including the honey cake.

4 oz icing sugar
4 oz butter
1 tablespoon of honey
4 tablespoons of lemon juice

Sift the icing sugar and cream it with the butter. Stir in the honey and lemon juice, beating it very well. This is then spread over the top of the cake. It has a nice, tart flavour. I usually have this one at Yule, as it is a nice cake to use then.

Apple Pie Variant

Take a good apple pie recipe and add ginger and dried fruit. It is something that we tradionally serve at the Beltane celebrations.

Apple Sponge Cake

Take a normal victoria sponge cake mix and add slices of apple. Put grease proof paper into your dish and then put the partly cooked apple slices into the cake dish. Add some ginger to your victoria sponge mixture, pour it over the apple and bake it according to your normal recipe. We sometimes have this at Beltane.

Herbs

Herb Vinegars

Another thing that I tend to do is to make my own vinegars. They are quite easy to make. Take herbs like fennel and coriander, the stronger tasting herbs, and put them into vinegar, just normal bottled vinegar, white vinegar preferably and just leave them there for a month or two, just giving it the occasional shake. You will find that the flavour comes out into the vinegar and they are really nice to use for salads.

Comfrey

Here is one recipe which uses comfrey instead of spinach.

Take, several handfuls of young washed shredded comfrey leaves half a cup of boiling water and 2 tablespoons of butter

Put the shredded leaves into boiling water, return to the boil, cover and cook until tender, about ten minutes. Drain it, add the butter and toss it well. It is nice served with minted new potatoes, but basically serve it as you want to, as a vegetable. Sometimes we put a few ground nuts on it too which is quite nice.

Hedgerow Fruits

During the Autumn months, there is a tremendous amount of wonderful fruit that can be gathered for free from the hedgerows. If you are going to gather things from the hedgerows, do not take things from the sides of roads due to the high amount of lead in the plants and berries. If you are going to gather, then do so from hedgerows in fields, preferably those used for grazing or 'set aside' and woods.

Elderberry Jam

The Elder tree, sacred to the Lady, gives us a marvellous crop of berries which not only make an excellent wine, but also this really tasty jam.

You want:

1 lb of berries to 1/4 pint of water
the juice of 2 lemons
1 lb of sugar

Boil it for 30 to 35 minutes until it sets when tested. You can take a small saucer of water and put a drop of the jam into the saucer. If it sets, that is, goes slightly hard, then it is ready. Put that into jars and fasten them down when it is cold. The jam will then set.

Apple and Elderberry Jelly

The good old elderberry can be used for so much in cooking and this jelly made by blending elderberries with apples is really good!

You want:

6 lbs of cooking apples
2 oz of elderberries
sugar

Wash the apples and cut into pieces. Strip the elderberries off the stems and place them with the apples in a preserving pan. Add sufficient cold water to cover the mixture. Bring the mixture to the boil, reduce the heat and simmer for about 45 minutes, or until the fruit is soft and pulpy. Strain it through a jelly bag. Measure one pound of sugar to each pint of juice. When the sugar has dissolved, boil rapidly until setting point is reached. Put it in warm jars and cover. This will give you about six pounds of jam.

Bramble jelly

Another excellent source of taste and nutrition from the hedgerows.

You will need:

4 lbs of blackberries, washed
10 fluid oz of water
2 tablespoons of lemon juice
some sugar

Place the blackberries, water and lemon juice in a preserving pan. Simmer it until the fruit is soft and pour the mixture into a jelly bag. Leave it for about twenty four hours, measure the juice and return it to a clean pan. Bring it to the boil and then reduce the heat. Add about one pound of sugar to each pint of juice. When the sugar has dissolved, boil it rapidly for about ten minutes, until setting point is reached. Get a small glass of water and drop some of the mixture into it. If it sets, then it is ready. Put it into warm jam jars and cover and label them. These quantites will yield about four pounds of jam. It is a very inexpensive way of making your jam for the year.

Crab Apple Jelly

You can sometimes find crab apples out in the wild, though they are easy to grow in the garden as well. These days you can even get crab apple trees which only need 2 feet of ground to grow in and do not need pruning at all!

If you can't get sufficient crab apples, they can be padded out with some cooking apples, or even saved peel and cores from cooking apples which help the jelly to set.

You want:

4 lb of crab apples
2 to 3 pints of cold water
rind of 2 lemons
sugar

Wash the apples and cut out any bad pieces. Quarter the apples and place them complete with peel and core in a large pan. Pour over enough cold water to cover the apples, add the lemon rind. Place the pan over a high heat and bring it to the boil. Reduce the heat to moderately low and simmer for an hour or until the apples are tender and mushy. Pour the apples and liquid into a jelly bag and leave overnight for the juice to strain into a pan.

Measure out the final amount of juice and pour it back into the pan. Add one pound of sugar to each pint of juice. Place the pan over a low heat and stir to dissolve the sugar. Increase the heat to high and bring the mixture to the boil. With a metal spoon, skim off any scum from the surface. Boil for ten minutes or until the setting point is reached. Remove the pan from the heat and let the jelly cool. Pour it into hot dry jam jars and label them. Store in a cool place. This should give you about three pounds of jam.

Sloe And Crab Apple Jelly

You want:

2 lb of sloes, trimmed and washed
1 lb of crab apples cut into quarters
the juice of one lemon
sugar

If you can't get crab apples, cooking apples can be used, though the jelly does not have quite the same flavour.

Using a large needle, prick the sloes all over and place them with the apples into a large saucepan. Add enough cold water to cover the fruit and add the lemon juice. Set the pan over a moderate heat, bringing the mixture to the boil. Reduce the heat to low and simmer for an hour or until the fruit is tender. Mash the fruit occasionally against the side of the pan with the back of a wooden spoon. Strain the sloes and the apple pulp into a jelly bag or cloth. Leave them for at least twelve hours or overnight.

When the juice has dripped through into the container, measure the juice and return it to the pan. Add a pound of sugar to every one pint of juice again. Set the pan over a low heat and cook, stirring until the sugar has dissolved. Increase the heat to high and bring the mixture to the boil. Boil briskly, without stirring for about ten minutes or until the jelly has reached setting point. Ladle the jelly into hot, clean, dry jars and label. This recipe will give you about eight pounds of jam.

Rosehip Syrup

I am going to finish off with a rose hip syrup. Rosehip syrup has been used for an awfully long time for children. It is a wonderful way of getting vitamin C. It also makes a refreshing summer's drink. You mix it with plenty of ice and a little water. It is very refreshing!

You need:

6 pints of water
4 lbs of ripe rosehips
2 oz sugar

Empty 6 pints of water into a large preserving pan and bring it to the boil. Wash and mince the rosehips and add them to the boiling water. Bring it back to the boil and remove it from the heat. Set it to one side and let it cool for about fifteen minutes. When it has cooled, pour it into a jelly bag and place it over a large mixing bowl. If you do not have a jelly bag, then a piece of muslin will do, preferably fine. Suspend it from a hook, over a bowl. Allow it to drain until all the juice has dripped through. Pour the juice into a clean pan. Bring it back to the boil and boil it until the juice reduces in quantity to about 3 pints. Reduce the heat to low and add the sugar. Simmer it until it is just dissolved. Remember to stir it frequently. Bring it back to the boil for a further five minutes and then pour the syrup into clean hot bottles.

Place your cork into the bottle as you would for wine and then dip it into wax so that you have a total seal. Then it should be able to keep for a short while. Once it is open though, it will only keep for a week or two. If possible, you want to bottle it into small bottles. As I said, it is a wonderful source of vitamin C for children. It is something that a lot of us have forgotten about. A lot of people used to use it, especially during the war, when children were employed to go out and pick the rose hips and were paid for them.

Alcohol

Another serious consideration in the Craft is alcohol - traditional at all our rituals. Whenever possible, we make our own. I have included a few traditional recipes. The first one is for mead.

Mead

This marvellous drink is steadily regaining the popularity it enjoyed years ago - with good reason!

The ingredients for mead are:

1 gallon of water
3 lbs of honey
2 ozs of bruised ginger
1 oz of fresh yeast

Boil the water for half an hour and add the honey and boil it for an hour again, skimming it if necessary to remove any impurities. Cut up the root ginger and bruise it. Put it into a small muslin bag and add it to the liquid. When it has cooled to hand hot add the fresh yeast. Put it into bottles and leave the corks loose until it has finished bubbling and then cork it tightly.

Mead is best left for at least six months to mature before drinking.

Lambswool

Now another drink that is consumed within the Craft, and is drunk a great deal by craftsfolk especially at Yule and Christmas is a very unusual drink called lambswool. Again, the only other place that I have found this drink is in Cornwall. It seems that an awful lot of the older recipes have survived down there. This is a sort of beer punch. This recipe should be enough for about eight people.

You need:

8 small apples
1 gallon of strong dark beer
1 inch pieces of cinnamon
6 cloves
6 allspice berries
A heaped tablespoon of brown sugar

Stick the cloves into the unpeeled apples and bake them in a little water in a hot oven, about 200C, until they are soft, but not till they are mushy. (That is important.) Just cook them until they are soft. Put them into a bowl, that is, the large bowl that you intend to serve the drink from. Put the beer, the spices and the sugar into a large saucepan and bring to just below boiling point.

Do not boil the beer, otherwise you will spoil the flavour and lose alcohol!

Pour that,through a strainer, over the apples and then serve it. We would normally have this with a hot spicy bread or cake. It is a lovely thing to have when you have just come in from the Yule celebrations and you are cold.

Elderberry Wine

This is an elderberry wine with a difference. I am not sure where I got the recipe from, but I have had it a long time.

You want to take 1 quart of berries to 2 quarts of water. Boil it for half an hour and then run the liquid and rub the fruit through a sieve. Then to every quart of juice, you want to add 3/4 lb of sugar.

Boil everything together for about 1/4 of an hour with some jamaican peppers and ginger and a few cloves. Pour it into a tub and when it has cooled down to hand warmth, pour it into the container that you are going to brew it in. Then you add, and this seems a very unusual thing to do, toast and yeast to work it. You want about an ounce to two ounces of yeast. You put that into the container and then you seal it with an air lock. You leave it to ferment. Once it has finished fermenting you put a quart of brandy to the eight gallons and then stop it up and bottle it and serve it after about six months - if you can wait that long.

Dandelion Wine.

Here is one that I cannot leave out. It is a good old fashioned recipe for dandelion wine. It is something that we would tend to drink in May, for Beltane because then it has had time to settle and mature during the winter.

You want:
3 quarts of freshly picked flower heads
3 lbs of sugar
1 oz of yeast
1 lb of raisins
1 gallon of water
The juice of 2 lemons

The juice of 1 orange

You put the flowers, without the green parts and stalks which are bitter, into a large bowl. Bring the water to the boil and pour over the dandelions. Leave it covered for three days. Stir it each day. On the third day, add the sugar and the rinds of the orange and lemons. Put it all into a pan and boil it for an hour. Return it to the boil and add the pulp of the lemons and orange. Leave it until it is a cool luke warm and then add the yeast. Let it remain covered for another three days and then it will be ready to strain and put into fermenting bottles. The fermenting bottles should not be quite full. The raisins should be divided equally amongst the fermentation bottles. Once it has finished fermenting you bottle the wine. If it is made in May or June, it should then be ready for Christmas. It can then be used as a Yule drink.

Rose Petal Wine

I know that there are an awful lot of wine recipes in here, but I am afraid that pagans at the best of times are an alcoholic bunch! Here is another one that would be nice to serve during the summer. It is rose wine.

You want:

1 1/2 lb of rose petals of one variety if possible
3 lbs of white sugar
1 lb of barley
1 oz of yeast
1 gallon of water

Boil the rose petals in half a gallon of water for fifteen minutes. Boil the barley in the other half gallon of water for five minutes. Leave them to cool and when they are both at blood temperature strain them into the sugar and stir until the sugar is dissolved. Cream the yeast in half a cup of warm water and add it to the mixture. Stir again and then pour into a demijohn which should then be sealed with an airlock. Leave it to ferment in a warm place for about a month. Once the bubbling has stopped, pour it into wine bottles through filter paper and cork them. Leave them for at least a year. Although it sounds a long time it is well worth doing.

Sloe Gin

Another thing that you will find out there is the sloe berry. I am going to give you the recipe for sloe gin, which I have to admit is something that we tend to make up for Christmas and it is lovely!

It is the fruit of the common blackthorn which you will find in most hedges and a lot of the woodlands. As I said, remember not to pick the ones by the roadside.

You will need:

1 lb of sloes, trimmed and washed
2 pints of gin
4 oz sugar
a few drops of almond essence

Using a large needle, prick the sloe berries all over. This will let a lot of flavour out into the gin. Place them in a large mixing bowl and pour the gin over them. Mix well and add the sugar and almond essence. Stir it well until it is blended. Pour the mixture into a large jug or crock and cork it tightly.

Set the jug aside in a dark place and allow the mixture to infuse for about three months, shaking it occasionally. Sterilise and dry two bottles. Pour the mixture through a funnel, lined with a very fine cheese cloth, into the bottles. Squeeze any pulp remaining in the cheese cloth with your hands, to extract the liquid. Discard the remaining pulp. Seal the bottles and set aside for at least six months before drinking.

Blackcurrant Gin

You can also make blackcurrant gin in the same way as for sloes, which is also very nice. It makes a highly enjoyable winter drink.

The Future Of The Earth
(The Day After Tomorrow)

The last part of this book is about the future of the Earth. There are many things happening in the world today. In many ways we are destroying it. Mostly, we do not mean to, but sometimes we take and do not think about what we are taking. The resources of this Earth will not be there for ever and we are gradually extinguishing them, be they animals that we can never replace or seas that we can never make clean again. We are destroying the Earth. Now is the time to do something about it. If each person who reads this book, just does one thing, just does something to stop it, then perhaps we have a chance.

Before you pick up that tin of cleaner, look at it. Is it biodegradable? That paper that you are about to throw away, if you put it in a separate stack and save it with other paper and take it along to be recycled, then that is one less part of a tree that has to be destroyed.

There is one particular group of people out there who are trying to do something for tomorrow and the government do not like them for it. The people that I am talking about in this country are called the Donga tribe. They are a group of people who came together to save the downland near Winchester, to try and stop the bulldozers from tearing through a very old hill for a motorway. That tribe is still together. They still work together. Whenever they are needed in the countryside, they go there and they protest and they are willing to lay down their lives for what they believe in. Perhaps there are too few people like them in the world and we need more of them.

The world needs more people to stand up against the governments and say, "No, we are not going to allow you to do this, we are not going to allow you to turn most of our countryside into motorways because you feel that is what we need. We do not need it." Do the governments truly do things for the people or themselves? They are people of power. They are meant to represent us. Do they truly do this?

In a way, in my spirit, I will be with the Donga wherever they are and try and help them in any way I can, even if it is to make sure that people do not forget that they are there and do not forget what they are doing.

Somebody called them the tribe of Albion. Yes, they are. One of the last tribes. Let us not forget the work that they do.

This country quite happily used razor wire to stop people gaining entry into areas where they are bulldozing and destroying the earth.

They say that over 5% of the countryside will be under tarmac within twenty five years. That includes sacred sites that cannot be replaced and ancient woods that cannot be regrown. Many of our sacred sites are falling under the bulldozer.

More and more the government want to fence them off so that we cannot touch them. Are they frightened of the power that these places hold? From the way that they unite people, I think so. We try to keep these sites with love. We do not try to destroy them.

Eighty five sacred sites are at this moment in danger of being bulldozed and covered over for roadways. That is far too many!

Look at individual countries and see what is happening. The American Indians are having to fight to save their sacred sites. The same in Canada. It seems that every single country is in danger of losing what they have.

Why? Because of man's greed.

Stand up and fight for what you believe in. Perhaps it is recycling. Perhaps it is finding a little local well and cleaning the rubbish and pollution away from it, cleaning it up and making it what it should be again. You could collect rubbish from sacred sites or places in the country that you might walk - take a bag with you when you walk. You are part of the community. Even if some communities refuse to take note that we are there, we still have a responsibility to what is around us and what will be there tomorrow for our children.

It is up to us today to save that, to make sure that there is a future in this country. I see people leaving the country because they think there is no future.

THE FUTURE IS WHAT WE MAKE OF IT.

Go to those sacred places. Tell them that you still love them and if they are in danger, work to save them.

The day after tomorrow, let us make sure that there is one, for the future of our children and theirs and the generations to come. Let it not be that we give them some sort of hell, where they can no longer swim in the sea or go for a walk in the country, because if we are not careful, that is how it is going to be.

I dedicate this last chapter to the Donga tribe, the children of Albion, the future, long may they fight and my spirit will always fight with them.

Thank You.

The Ending

This in a way, is a small piece before the end, to say things and to talk about things that do concern me in the world that we live in today.

Many of us try to rush things. We try to run before we can walk. That is not what this book has been about. This book has been designed to work over a year, a year of your life. During the past year, I have seen many things, some things that have distressed me that man is doing to man.

I have seen a part of the countryside that I used to love and a place that I sometimes used to work, a place just outside Winchester, a place beside the hill called St. Catherines. I have seen a group of young people come together to fight for that area, to fight for what they believe in. I mentioned them earlier in this book, the Donga tribe. I have seen their flame live and I have seen their flame grow.

Just as their flame is growing, there are many other tribes in this country that are growing. They are not the only tribe now in this land. There are many. There are many who are now coming together and saying,"We have a religion and it is a religion that we believe in. It is a religion that we have a right to". I see their strength grow and I see their love and companionship grow. Then I look outside this country and I see the war and the things that are going on around us. If each of us, in our own way can do something, we can help. All I ask is that you think what you can do to help.

The end of any book is very difficult. What to say? I have tried to help give you a guide to the basics, to the everyday parts and to help, I hope to open you up to what is inside us all. Everyone has the possibility, everyone has it within themselves to open up to what is around them. Many books that I have seen on the market start with the fact that they think that you already know everything that there is to know. I hope this book has given you some basic pointers, some ideas, some clear thoughts as to what the worship of the God and Goddess are about.

It is not just about rituals and celebrations, it is about feelings, the feelings within us all. During the years and my time in the Craft, I have met many people, I have touched their lives and moved on. In a way, I feel that through this book, I have touched yours. We most probably will never meet. You may just read these words and decide that this way is not for you. Or you may decide that yes, I want to go on.

I hope that this book has given you the chance, has given you ideas and inspiration. There are many times and many occasions that I can tell you about, but there is not enough time here.

The pathway is a special one. It brings love and laughter and happiness into your life. It will also bring times of pain, even of disaster, but the good times outweigh the bad. In my life I could never see a time without the presence of the Lord and Lady. In many ways now, they are my life. They are my love and my soul.

I have been faced many times on the pathway with occasions when I thought I should leave the pathway, but each time I come back, because I find that their message within my heart is still strong, it is still there. I myself have learned a lot, I have found out a lot about myself through my journey and I know that in the times ahead, you may have to face parts of you that you may not enjoy. You may have to face up to things, responsibilities that you would much rather not face up to. But in taking the Lord and Lady into your life, you also know that they are there with you. They are there walking the pathway.

It is now time for me to leave, to leave your life in what you have read. We have walked along the same pathway for quite a while. I hope that through what I have written, you have learned something. Though I may leave the pathway, there are two other people beside you on that pathway, the Lord and the Lady. So I will leave you now in their care and with their love.

In many ways, I do not wish to say goodbye. It is funny that although I have never met you, I feel that I know you. I can see you sitting there reading this book, or perhaps, you are like me and have picked up a book and have turned to the very end to see how the book ends. For you, I will give a simple message. Start at the beginning. It is the only way in the end! You will gain nothing by skipping pages, because every page has something to say. Every word has been thought out carefully.

I hope that perhaps, one day, we will meet and if we do, then may there be joy in our meeting.

May the Mother smile on you and may the Father bless your spirit.

Goodbye.

A selection of other titles from Capall Bann:

Available through your local bookshop, or direct from Capall Bann at: Freshfields, Chieveley, Berks, RG16 8TF.

West Country Wicca - A Journal of the Old Religion By Rhiannon Ryall

This book is a valuable and enjoyable contribution to contemporary Wicca. It is a simple account of the Old Religion. The portrayal of Wicca in the olden days is at once charming and deeply religious, combining joy, simplicity and reverence. The wisdom emanating from country folk who live close to Nature shines forth from every page - a wisdom which can add depth and colour to our present day understanding of the Craft. Without placing more value on her way than ours, Rhiannon provides us with a direct path back to the Old Religion in the British Isles. *This is how it was*, she tells us. *This is the way I remember it.* Both the content of what she remembers and the form in which she tells us, are straightforward, homespun and thoroughly unaffected.

"West Country Wicca is a real gem - it is the best book on witchcraft I have ever seen! Thank you Rhiannon Ryall for sharing your path with us." - Marion Weinstein

ISBN Number   1 89830 702 4   Price £7.95

The Call of the Horned Piper by Nigel Aldcroft Jackson

This book originated as a series of articles, later much expanded, covering the symbolism, archetypes and myths of the Traditional Craft (or Old Religion) in the British Isles and Europe. The first section of the book explores the inner symbology and mythopoetics of the old Witchcraft religion, whilst the second part gives a practical treatment of the sacred sabbatic cycle, the working tools, incantations, spells and pathworking. There are also sections on spirit lines, knots and thread lore and ancestral faery teachings. Extensively illustrated with the author's original artwork. This is a radical and fresh re-appraisal of authentic witch-lore which may provide a working alternative to current mainstream trends in Wicca.

ISBN Number   1-898307-09-1   Price £8.95

The Sacred Grove - The Mysteries of the Tree By Yvonne Aburrow

The veneration of trees was a predominant theme in the paganism of the Romans, Greeks, Celtic & Germanic peoples. Many of their rites took place in sacred groves & much of their symbolism involved the cosmic tree; its branches supported the heavens, its trunk was the centre of the earth & its roots penetrated the underworld. This book explains the various mysteries of the tree & explains how these can be incorporated into modern paganism. This gives a new perspective on the cycle of seasonal festivals & the book includes a series of rituals incorporating tree symbolism. "The Sacred Grove" is the companion volume to "The Enchanted Forest - The Magical Lore of Trees, but can be read in its own right as an exploration of the mysteries of the tree.

ISBN Number 1 898307 12 1   Price £10.95

Angels & Goddesses - Celtic Paganism & Christianity
by Michael Howard
This book traces the history and development of Celtic Paganism and Celtic Christianity specifically in Wales, but also in relation to the rest of the British Isles including Ireland, during the period from the Iron Age, through to the present day. It also studies the transition between the old pagan religions & Christianity & how the early Church, especially in the Celtic counmtries, both struggled with & later absorbed the earlier forms of spirituality it encountered. The book also deals with the way in which the Roman Catholic version of Christianity arrived in south-east England & the end of the 6th century, when the Pope sent St. Augustine on his famous mission to convert the pagan Saxons, & how this affected the Celtic Church.. It discusses how the Roman Church suppressed Celtic Christianity & the effect this was to have on the history & theology of the Church during the later Middle Ages. The influence of Celtic Chhristianity on the Arthurian legends & the Grail romances is explored as well as surviving traditions of Celtic bardism in the medieval period. The conclusion on the book covers the interest in Celtic Christianity today & how, despite attempts to eradicate it from the pages of clerical history, its ideas & ideals have managed to survive & are now influencing New Age concepts & are relevent to the critical debate about the future of the modern chrurch.

ISBN 1-898307-03-2 Price £9.95

Auguries and Omens - The Magical Lore of Birds By Yvonne Aburrow
The folklore & mythology of birds is central to an understanding of the ancient world, yet it is a neglected topic. This book sets out to remedy this situation, examining in detail the interpretation of birds as auguries & omens, the mythology of birds (Roman, Greek, Celtic & Teutonic), the folklore & weather lore associated with them, their use in heraldry & falconry & their appearances in folk songs & poetry. The book examines these areas in a general way, then goes into specific details of individual birds from the albatross to the yellowhammer, including many indigenous British species, as well as more exotic & even mythical birds.

ISBN Number 1 898307 11 3   Price £10.95

The Pickingill Papers - The Origin of the Gardnerian Craft by W. E. Liddell
Compiled & Edited by Michael Howard
George Pickingill (1816 - 1909) was said to be the leader of the witches in Canewdon, Essex. In detailed correspondence with 'The Wiccan' & 'The Cauldron' magazines from 1974 - 1994, E. W. Liddell, claimed to be a member of the 'true persuasion', i.e. the Hereditary Craft. He further claimed that he had relatives in various parts of southern England who were coven leaders & that his own parent coven (in Essex) had been founded by George Pickingill's grandfather in the 18th century. There is considerable interest in the material in the so-called 'Pickingill Papers' & the controversy still rages about their content & significance with regard to the origins of Gardnerian Wicca. This book provides, for the first time, a chance for the complete Pickingill material to be read & examined in toto together with background references & extensive explanatory notes. Topics included in this book include the origin of the Gardnerian Book of Shadows and Aleister Crowley's involvement, the relationship between the Hereditary Craft, Gardnerian Wicca & Pickingill's Nine Covens, the influence of Freemasonry on the medieval witch cult, sex magic, ley lines & earth energy, prehistoric shamanism, the East Anglian lodges of cunning men, the difference between Celtic wise women & the Anglo Saxon cunning men. It also includes new material on the Craft Laws, the New Forest coven, Pickingill's influence on the Revived Craft & a refutation of the material on Lugh & his basic thesis in Aidan Kelly's recent book 'Crafting the Art of Magic'.

ISBN Number 1 898307 10 5   Price £9.95

The Inner Space Work Book By Cat Summers & Julian Vayne

A detailed, practical book on psychic and personal development using the Tarot, pathworkings and meditations. The Inner Space Work Book provides a framework for developing your psychic and magickal abilities; exploring techniques as varied as shamanism, bodymind skills and ritual, through the medium of the tarot. There are two interwoven pathways through the text. One concentrates on the development of psychic sensitivity, divination and counselling, as well as discussing their ethics and practical application. The second pathway leads the student deeper into the realm of Inner Space, exploring the Self through meditation, pathworking, physical exercises and ritual. Both paths weave together to provide the student with a firm grounding in many aspects of the esoteric. Together, the pathways in The Inner Space Work Book, form a 'user friendly' system for unlocking all your latent magickal talents.

ISBN 1 898307 13 X   Price £9.95

Pathworking 2nd Ed. By Pete Jennings & Pete Sawyer

A pathworking is, very simply, a guided meditational exercise, it is sometimes referred to as 'channelling' or 'questing'. It is used for many different aims, from raising consciousness to healing rituals You don't have to possess particular beliefs or large sums of money to benefit from it & it can be conducted within a group or solo at time intervals to suit you. This book teaches you how to alter your conscious state, deal with stress, search for esoteric knowledge or simply have fun & relax. It starts with a clear explanation of the theory of pathworking and shows in simple & concise terms what it is about and how to achieve results, then goes on to more advanced paths & how to develop your own, it also contains over 30 detailed and explained pathworkings. Highly practical advice & information is given on how to establish and manage your own group. No previous experience is assumed.

ISBN Number   1 898307 00 8   Price £7.95

Celtic Lore & Druidic Ritual By Rhiannon Ryall

Rhiannon Ryall is well known for her book 'West Country Wicca'. This new book brings some of the inner mysteries to those interested in the Pagan Path or Tradition. Inevitably the Druidic Path crosses that of any genuine Gaelic Tradition of Wicca, so this book contains much druidic lore.. Background material pertaining to the Druids is also included as this explains much of their way of viewing the world and it enables the reader to understand more fully their attributions in general and their rituals in particular. The book is divided into five parts:

1: Casting circles, seasonal sigils, wands, woods for times of the year, Celtic runes, the Great Tides, making cones and vortices, polarities and how to change them, the seasonal Ogham keys and some Ogham correspondences. 2: Old calendar festivals and associated evocations, the "Call of Nine", two versions of the 'Six pointed Star Dance', Mistletoe Lore, New Moon working,the Fivefold Calendar. 3: Underlying fundamentals of magical work, magical squares and their applications, more use of Oghams, the Diamond Working area. 4: Five initiations, including a shamanic one, some minor 'calls', some 'little magics'. 5: Background information on the Celtic path, the Arthurian myth and its underlying meaning and significance, the Three Worlds of the Celts, thoughts regarding the Hidden Path, some thoughts and final advice. A veritable treasure trove for anyone interested in the Celtic path.

ISBN 1 898307 225   Price £9.95

The Mysteries of the Runes By Michael Howard

The book follows the historical development of the runes from earlier Neolithic & Bronze Age alphabets & symbols & their connection with other magical & mystical symbols including the swastika, sunwheel, equal-armed cross etc. Historical references to the runes & their use in divination by Germanic tribes & the Saxons together with the Viking use of the runes in Dark Age Engl& are also covered. The Norse god Odin is discussed, as the shaman-god of the runes together with his associated myths, legends & folklore, the Wild Hunt, the Valkyries & his connections with the Roman god Mercury, the Egyptian god Thoth, Jesus & the Odinic mysteries. The magical uses of the runes are described, their use in divination with examples of their everyday use. Fascinating information is included on the runes discovered during archaelogical excavations, rune masters & mistresses, the bog sacrifices of Sc&anavia & the training of the rune master, both ancient & modern.

The symbolism and detailed descriptions of each of the eight runes of Freya's Aett, Haegl's Aett & Tyr's Aett are given with divinity, religious symbolism & spiritual meanings etc based on The Anglo Saxon Rune Poem. Details on how to make your own set of runes are included, how to cast the runes for divination with examples of readings &suggested layouts & the use of rune magic. The final section covers Bronze Age Sc&anavia & its religious belief systems; the gods & goddess of the Aesir & Vanir, their myths & legends & the seasonal cycle of festivals in the Northern Tradition. Also discussed are the Web of Wyrd & the Norns, Saxon/Norse paganism & traditional witchcraft.

ISBN Number   1-898307-07-0   Price £8.95

The Enchanted Forest - The Magical Lore of Trees By Yvonne Aburrow

This is a truly unique book covering the mythology, folklore, medicinal & craft uses of trees. Associated rhymes & songs are also included together with the esoteric correspondences - polarity, planet, deity, rune & Ogham. There is a short history of tree lore, its purpose & applications. A further section gives information on tree spirits & their importance. The text is profusely illustrated with line drawings by the author & artist Gill Bent. This book will appeal to anyone who likes trees.

ISBN Number   1-898307-08-3   Price £10.95

In Search of Herne the Hunter   By Eric Fitch

The book commences with an introduction to Herne's story & his relationship with Windsor, the oak on which Herne hanged himself & its significance in history & mythology. The next section investigates antlers & their symbology in prehistoric religions, together with a study of the horned god Cernunnos, the Wild Hunt & its associations with Woden, Herne etc. & the Christian devil. There is a descriptive chapter on the tradition of dressing up as animals & the wearing & use of antlers in particular. Herne's suicide & its connection with Woden & prehistoric sacrifice is covered, together with the most complete collection of Herne's appearances, plus an investigation into the nature of his hauntings. The final section brings all the strands together, plus some additional material. Photographs, illustrations & diagrams enhance the authoritative & well researched text. The book also contains appendices covering the 19th century opera on the legend of Herne, Herne & his status in certain esoteric circles & Herne & Paganism/Wicca.

Price £9.95   ISBN 1 898307 237   Publication date July 1994

Capall Bann Publishing is owned & run by people with experience & beliefs in the fields in which they publish. New titles are constantly being added to the range, full details are available on request.